*Systemic Psychotherapy
with Families, Couples,
and Individuals*

Systemic Psychotherapy with Families, Couples, and Individuals

by Guido L. Burbatti, M.D., Ph.D.,
Ivana Castoldi, and Lucia Maggi

translated by Carolyn Shor Novick

Jason Aronson Inc.
Northvale, New Jersey
London

Production editor: Judith D. Cohen

This book was set in 11 point Palacio by Lind Graphics of Upper Saddle River, New Jersey, and printed and bound by Haddon Craftsmen in Scranton, Pennsylvania.

Library of Congress Cataloging-in-Publication Data

Burbatti, Guido L., , 1945–
    Systemic psychotherapy with families, couples, and individuals /
by G. Burbatti, I. Castoldi, and L. Maggi.
        p. cm.
    Includes bibliographical references and index.
    ISBN 0-87668-390-1
    1. Psychotherapy patients—Family relationships.
2. Psychotherapy. 3. Family—Psychological aspects. 4. Family
psychotherapy. I. Castoldi, I. (Ivana) II. Maggi, L. (Lucia)
III. Title.
RC489.F33B87 1993
616.89′14—dc20   92-9280

Manufactured in the United States of America. Jason Aronson Inc. offers books and cassettes. For information and catalog write to Jason Aronson Inc., 230 Livingston Street, Northvale, New Jersey 07647.

To our children

Gertrude

Annalisa

Chiara

Francesca

Jacopo

Verily you are suspended like scales between your sorrow and your joy. Only when you are empty are you at standstill and balanced.

Kahlil Gibran, *The Prophet*

CONTENTS

PREFACE

This book was written to describe the clinical work of the past five years that inspired us to devise the systemic therapy model that our hospital is currently using. It is the sequel to our book *The Milan Approach to Family Therapy*. The evolution of the clinical model is the fruit of our continuing reflections on theory and therapeutic experience which, by definition, are characterized by temporariness and subject to revision.

The Milan Approach was the most precise description possible of a therapeutic model that seemed, to others as well as us, to be a conceptual heir of the original MRI (Mental Research Institute) group of Palo Alto, because while we adhered very strictly to their Batesonian epistemology, we had a novel and consistent manner in which we utilized the Palo Alto model in our clinical practice.

Over the years we have done much clinical work using the Milan Approach. Although our results seemed satisfactory to us, we gradually became aware that we could no longer rigidly, if consistently, apply this model in our clinical practice. At first we thought that this was due to a change in the current types of mental disorder. We felt that the social, economic, and cultural world around us was changing at a dizzying speed, and we would therefore be confronting new types of psychological illness that would be more complex to study and understand as well as more difficult to treat. At this same time, we were captivated by theoretical debate going on in the field with regard to epistemology. This gradually undermined our certainty in defining ourselves as Milan Approach systemic therapists. We found we were not practicing what we were preaching and blaming change in the prevailing types of mental illness for the increasing difficulties we encountered and for any lack of success we experienced in resolving cases.

Without any of us consciously deciding to do this, we began making various changes in our work with families. At the time, we excused these departures from routine practice as exceptions that prove the rule. For example, we began to deal with cases of anorexia and psychosis on parallel levels. In some cases, we would work with the family and have a colleague do individual therapy with the identified patient. In other cases, we would limit our work with the family to one or two diagnostic consultation sessions and continue individual therapy with the patient. These and other innovations were rather unorthodox departures from the Milan Approach.

As time passed, we began to realize that our clinical work had undergone quite a transformation and that its tendency was in a direction further and further away from our original theoretical model. We were coming closer and closer to what we had already for some time asserted on a theoretical level, which is that human systems do not behave according to the input–output model, but instead are autonomous systems.

This book is our attempt to describe the change that we have undergone, particularly in our clinical work with families and with individual patients. We feel that this work is one step beyond with respect to the evolution that the traditional systemic epistemology has undergone in the past decade (in other fields as well as in our own), passing from first-order to second-order cybernetics.

It is also our first attempt to demonstrate the possibility of using the systemic model (that was created for and traditionally used for family therapy) in individual therapy, and thus to elaborate a general model of systemic psychotherapy.

We would like to thank everyone who, directly or indirectly, contributed to the draft of this book.

First of all, my personal thanks go to Dr. Jason Aronson for the faith that he has shown in the work of our group and for his persistent requests that we write about what we were doing.

The credit for having given us very valuable help in bibliographical research and having organized the bibliography for each section goes to Dr. Giovanni Bernardini and Dr. Erasmo Scavazza.

Dr. Anna Armati, using her computer know-how, gave us technical help in the phase of assembling the manuscript. Along with Dr. Scavazza, she managed to put order into our disorganization, retrieving various sections scattered in a hodgepodge of files and programs.

The students of our School of Professional Training in Systemic Therapy Theory and Practice, with their constant interest and curiosity about the theoretical aspects of the model, were a precious source of stimulation to us.

To Dr. Carolyn Shor Novick, the translator of our book, sincere thanks for having adapted her work rhythms to ours, even giving up vacation time to finish the work on schedule.

Each of us wishes to thank our co-authors for contributing to the growth of our group and for sharing with us, even in difficult moments, the enthusiasm necessary to create this work.

Last but not least, we would like to recognize, with deep affection and gratitude, all of those who, by confiding their sufferings to us, made it possible for us, too, to grow and make progress toward achieving our goals.

Guido Burbatti
Milan, April 1992

Part 1 | **THE PAST**

FROM LINEAR TO
Chapter 1 | # SYSTEMIC THINKING

Before presenting our clinical model and illustrating various aspects of it, it is necessary that we indicate the theories (as well as their authors) that are pertinent to our work. We initiated our collaboration as the new staff of the Centro per lo Studio e la Terapia della Famiglia at Niguarda Hospital in Milan, Italy at the end of the 1970s.

To reconstruct the itinerary of our thinking, it is necessary to return and pass through the stages of a decade-long journey that began with our use of a causal and linear theoretical model and that led us progressively toward a systemic and complex mode of thinking.

The initial phase of our study of systems was based on the general system theory of von Bertalanffy and on von Neumann-type cybernetic models. During this period we adhered to the "epistemology of representation." It was characterized by many attempts to construct models, in various academic fields, that ideally would become closer and closer to being isomorphous with reality. These models were to be used to represent the reality that was thought to be the basis of the world of phenomena, that is, a reality not directly knowable, but nonetheless describable. For us, as systemic family therapists, the reality to know and to describe was, of course, that of human systems and of family systems.

Nonetheless, we were also aware of the impossibility of arriving at an absolute, objective knowledge, because our representations of reality were relative and dependent upon the observer. Already, Bateson (1979) had warned that science is a way of perceiving reality that is limited by its explorative methods to gathering the outward and visible signs of what might be reality. Bateson also said that every experience is subjective because it is the brain that constructs the images that we believe we are perceiving. Bateson's conviction that it is impossible for living systems to gather objective information about their physical environment is borne out by important research on perception conducted at the end of the 1950s by McCulloch and colleagues (1965).

It was not long before our conviction that it was possible to represent or describe reality, albeit in a subjective manner, began to waver. Research in the field of neurophysiology (in particular Maturana 1980, Maturana and Varela 1980, 1985, Varela 1979, 1985) had demonstrated that the nervous system works as a closed system, that is, it does not contain representations or codified versions of the outside world (Maturana and Varela 1980, 1985). In addition, these studies on biological systems contributed to the definition of basic concepts such as autopoiesis, structural determinism, and organizational closure. Like other systemic therapists, we began to use these concepts more and more to illustrate the basic laws of how living systems function.

Research concerning new models of artificial intelligence as well as studies in cell biology and in neurophysiology also demonstrated the properties of self-organization and self-reference in autonomous systems. Naturally, these are also properties of living systems, autonomous systems par excellence.

These new theoretical conceptualizations profoundly changed our view with regard to the study of systems. We progressed from the idea of a given reality to describe to the idea of a "reality" to construct together by interaction with other systems. In effect, we passed from a first-order cybernetics paradigm to a second-order cybernetics paradigm (Sluzky 1986), thus following the same spontaneous evolution that characterized all of the sciences, even the human and social sciences, during the 1980s.

The way in which the mechanism of functioning of a living or social system was described up until about a decade ago, that is, from the point of view of first-order cybernetics, seems extremely reductive nowadays. At that time, the experts in cybernetics had models that were certainly valid for deterministic electronic computers, but they were not adequate for describing the processes of self-organization that characterize nondeterministic computers with artificial intelligence, and they certainly were not adequate for describing the activities of living systems. However, these were the only models that were available at that time.

It was the inadequacy of these models that stimulated us, even at the very beginning of our work as clinical researchers. In addition, the awareness of the necessity to formulate a precise definition of *system* that would be valid in our field of study pervaded our theoretical reflections. Even if the definition of system can be reduced to a mathematical formula in the exact sciences, this is not the case in the fields of medicine, biology, or the social sciences. For this reason, we found ourselves confronted by the necessity to redefine, in the field of psychology, concepts borrowed from other domains.

The first phase of our multidisciplinary research was marked by the idea of a system as a whole to be broken up into parts and subsequently recomposed by means of simple operations, which then, as a sum, generated a complex activity. This was the phase of theoretical research, which occupied the attention of our group for a number of years in the attempt to work out a detailed formulation of the clinical model that we were using at the time. We worked in collaboration with the Institute of Cybernetics at the Università degli Studi in Milan, attending seminars and study groups. The clinical model that was the basis for our original therapeutic approach was that of the Milan School of Selvini, Boscolo, Cecchin, and Prata, where some members of our staff were trained.

The first definition of system that we dealt with was derived from the scientific organization of work. The factory, with its form of organization, was considered the system par excellence. Its complex activities were broken down into simple basic activities that could be carried out by assembly lines. It was thus possible to put together a definition of system expressed graphically by a series of blocks.

The image of the "black box" (Watzlawick et al. 1967) illustrates Taylor's (1947) conception of system, and it was the source of the simplest system in a paradigm of control. The system works in this manner: there is an input, then some sort of signal or flow of energy is emitted inside the black box (whose laws of functioning are purposely ignored), and then there is a predictable output.

This model was refined with the introduction of the flow chart, invented by von Neumann. It is a diagram that illustrates the functioning of the various activities of the system. (On a practical level, the flow chart could be used to describe symbolically the actions to be carried out during a therapeutic session!)

The idea of feedback made it possible to insert into the model the capacity for regulation of the processes of functioning of the black box. Regulation keeps the characteristic variables of the system within the limits that are compatible with its survival, and avoids runaway.

This model of first-order cybernetics, applied to the systems that were (and still are) the object of our research, appeared more and more inadequate in the light of our experience.

First of all, in a system that is described as a black box, the parts are not autonomous, and moreover, they are not distinguished one from another as parts of the whole. On the other hand, what we have learned during the course of our clinical and theoretical work is that in natural and biological systems, such as social systems, the autonomy of the parts makes for complexity by means of interactions and reciprocal coordination. Therefore, for us, a biological or social system is really a complex entity in which the parts affect the whole and the whole acts upon the parts in a circular process (Morin 1980).

Moreover, we have seen in our work that the autonomy of living systems guarantees the possibility of spontaneous evolution, utilizing even positive feedback (amplification of the deviation). This conceptualization frees us from the preconception that the survival of a system depends on the possibility of its being controlled, in the sense of regulation, by means of homeostatic processes of minimization, and it opens new perspectives with regard to the possibilities of change within the system itself.

All of these reflections pushed us toward new horizons, causing us to abandon the too-simplistic model of the black box. In the mid-eighties, we began to work on the paradigm of autopoiesis, organizing in our Center a multidisciplinary group of diverse types of professionals (psychiatrists, psychologists, a biologist, and a physicist). Working in this way, we passed from the study of single-celled and multi-celled biological systems and autopoietic first- and second-order systems (Maturana and Varela 1980) to social systems.

In this phase of our theoretical research, one controversial topic, debated at length, had to do with the possibility of defining *family system* in autopoietic terms. At the beginning, we attempted to transfer the concept of autopoiesis from a physical domain to a linguistic domain, that is, the domain of the unique relationships of social systems. Later on, we abandoned this attempt because it did not seem correct to us to equate autonomy with autopoiesis. The organization of a social system, such as a family, does not come into being through the physical and chemical production of its components, the way biological systems do, and its limits are not of a topological nature.

Recursive relations of a linguistic nature guarantee self-reference in family systems, and, therefore, also guarantee their autonomy without it being necessary to speak of autopoiesis. All of these reflections, developed during the course of these years, were gradually directing us toward a different point of view.

Subsequently, particularly in the second half of the 1980s, the evolution of our thinking was influenced by the developments in the epistemology of complexity and by the research in synergetics, all of which rapidly changed our theoretical and clinical point of view.

One could say, then, that our current thinking has its roots in two distinct periods of our history. The more remote past is connected with our research on systems in a paradigm of control and with our fidelity to the Milan Approach as it was presented in the early writings of Selvini's group (Selvini

Palazzoli et al. 1978). This is the model that we have adapted and revised, rather substantially with regard to some aspects. However, the more recent past is part of the history that we intend to illustrate in this book. It is the period of our study of the epistemology of complexity and of the theory of the autonomy of living systems. It is the phase of our search for a new conceptualization of the family system and for the creation of a new way of doing therapy. We would like briefly to retrace this part of our history to point out the path that brought us, sometimes in a roundabout way, to our current theoretical and practical knowledge.

Chapter 2 | **THE FAMILY SYSTEM**

BOUNDARIES AND ORGANIZATION

The definition of *family system* engaged our minds for quite some time. The decision to set about defining family system in functional terms, that is, a family as a group of individuals living together under the same roof, responded to a practical need. The first step in our clinical practice is handled by the nurse who gathers information from the family member who has telephoned the center for an appointment. Since the nurse must ask the whole family to come, it was necessary for us to decide what we meant by family or family system (Burbatti and Formenti 1988).

However, this definition, which we would call a practical one, cannot be generalized. It happens quite often that we decide, after the first consultation session, to summon members who do not live together with the rest of the family, but who, nonetheless, participate in the organization of the family. Similarly, sometimes we feel that it is useful to dismiss a component of the family in order to conduct therapy with a subsystem.

We agreed, in any case, to maintain the usual convocation

procedure, even though we were aware that we would have to take into consideration the boundaries of the system that came to the first session, perhaps deciding to expand them or to contract them. After long discussion, we came to the conclusion that an unequivocal definition of family was impossible as well as unacceptable on theoretical grounds. All that one could do was to set up practical criteria, which, of course, had to be relative and flexible, while making a distinction between the system to convoke for the first session and the system that would receive therapeutic treatment.

Since we are dealing with a social system, the boundaries are defined in a *nonreal* domain, that is, not in a physical, but in a linguistic one: the area of the observations and descriptions shared by different observers on the basis of their common experience. This consideration brings to mind an epistemological problem that makes our operative definition of family system even more relative. A system does not exist per se in the absolute unless there is an observer who individuates it, distinguishing it from an undifferentiated background. Thus, the observer performs operations that Varela (1979) defines as *distinction* and *indication*. It is possible, then, that different observers individuate different systems from the same ground. Only a sharing of common theoretical principles, observation techniques, and professional tools allows for creating a consensual domain among the observers and makes it possible to formulate a definition of system. Obviously, such a definition refers to the recognition of the special organization of the system with which we are working at the time and with which we are interacting. The concept of a different system's boundaries and of its organization are therefore closely connected, although not necessarily perfectly identical. The first one is correlative to the second, and vice versa.

Even the definition of the organization of the system, so important because it specifies its identity, is a thorny problem, because it is impossible to produce a definition that is unequivocal. Again, we have to keep in mind the observer and his/her epistemological lenses. Potentially, there are as many definitions as there are observers. We stress the power of the observer to produce arbitrary descriptions and the necessity to find a domain of common criteria shared with other observers. Thus, because the discrimination of and definition of the boundaries and organization of a system are produced by the linguistic consenus of a community of observers, they will remain constant as long as the generative conditions of the given system remain unchanged.

Hoping to make the above concept clearer, we will illustrate it with an extreme example.

Let us imagine the ludicrous situation in which the organization of a family, which we will call the Brown family, is formed around the fact that all of its members have the same occupation: they are managers in a fabric store. We note that this store has been handed down from generation to generation, creating a real tradition, the development of particular communicative and relational patterns among the family members. Obviously, it would be difficult to restrict the boundaries of the Brown family to the nuclear family. In fact, they could just as well include the grandparents, who are still associated with the business. From this point of view, we could think that the system would not undergo any change as long as the situation remains the same. But if one day Bill, the eldest son, decided to leave the business and go to work for a computer company, what would happen? It is logical to suppose that the Browns would not be the Browns of before. In other words, the family would encounter a perturbation that could have a marked effect on its organization, leaving its boundary lines drastically changed. Bill might well be considered, in practical terms, no longer a member of the family, except in terms of the irrevocable blood relationship that ties him to his parents and his siblings.

Fortunately for us, the breakdown of the organization of a social system does not coincide with the death of its component members, as happens in other autonomous systems, such as a cell or a multicellular system. Following a perturbation, a social system could again set up the same type of organization that it had had in the past, or else it could change types. Its boundaries could shrink or they could expand by taking on other components. To return to our example, the plasticity of the family could even allow for the reentry of Bill in a subsequent phase of development.

THE COMPONENTS OF THE SYSTEM

For quite some time, family therapists suffered from a sort of selective myopia (in the most pernicious cases, from a kind of blindness): they could see only families. The individuals who made up the families were reduced to mere shadows in the background, or they were even considered nonexistent. We think that what occurred had to do with an error in interpreting the underlying basic theoretical models, in this case, the general system theory of von Bertalanffy (von Bertalanffy 1969). The fundamental premise that a system as a whole is something different from the mere sum of its parts stresses the complexity of the dynamics of the makeup of a system. It is dependent on the totality, but it does not deny the existence of the parts (in our case, individuals), which are endowed with characteristics that become evident through reciprocal interactions.

In the same way, we could ask ourselves why it is that family therapists have translated the idea of the "irrelevance of the intrapsychic," historically expressed by the School of Palo Alto (Watzlawick et al. 1967) as the "irrelevance of the individual." It seems to us that the nonpertinence of the operation is evident (Watzlawick et al. 1967).

As a consequence of our rethinking this matter, we began, at first on a theoretical level congruent with the systemic model with which we identify, to restore the individual as an integral part of the network of processes that account for the existence of the family system. In a successive phase, this recovery also involved the area of clinical practice, producing changes in the technique of the conducting of family therapy sessions, as well as drawing us closer to the practice of individual therapy. (See the sections on the present and the future in this book.) Terms such as *identity, role definition,* and *consciousness* reappeared in our vocabulary, albeit in relational and social terms.

We think of the family as a structural union of the third order, composed of second-order systems, that is, the individuals who make up this whole (Varela 1989).

The various relationships of different intensity and types between the members of the family could be described as a system of ideas in common that are sufficiently stable over an arc of time to give rise to networks of behaviors and to common ideas, such as who we are, who is a family member, which behaviors are permitted, which roles are filled by which members, and so forth. All of this acts as a sort of glue, determining, among other things, a particular physiognomy of the system.

Another attribute of the individual is that of being able to be included, either contemporaneously or in successive moments, in various systems, participating in diverse relational networks. This brings about the emergence of a plurality of identities. By *identity* we mean that structure through which the individual becomes the object of his/her own autoperception. It has to do with a symbolic representation, recognized by others and by himself/herself, made possible by the use of language. Thus, for the concept of identity (or self), we emphasize the aspect of its social evolution (Mead 1934).

Thus, if a person is at the same time father, husband, company manager, and patient of a psychotherapist, he would have the identities of parent, marriage partner, manager, and so on. The individual is the central point and the node of the interaction network that connects these different identities. Obviously, when one of these identities is lost, the person still survives, even though this loss might cause repercussions in some or all of the systems of which this person is a component. The idea that certain events that take place out of the family system cause important restructurings within the family system, and vice versa, is so taken for granted as to seem almost banal.

Individuals and the systems that are made up of them produce intense activity of linguistic coordination, but this does not necessarily mean that the individual is aware of his/her own relational involvement, the specific role played, and the conditions of participation in his/her own system. This possibility, which Maturana (1980) calls *social consciousness*, is not a direct consequence of language, even though it is made possible by the use of language. Although one participates in communication networks, it is quite possible to be unaware of these conditions. To become aware, it is necessary that the individual become the observer of himself/herself, of his/her social reality, and of the environment in which he/she lives.

This leads us to the area of psychotherapy, in which it is often the therapist's job to construct, together with the family, a domain of metadescriptions that can make evident each component's position in the network of relationships that connects them to each other in more or less pathological terms.

AREAS OF OBSERVATION-INTERACTION OF A FAMILY SYSTEM

The family system becomes clear to us at the termination of a complex operation of distinction performed by one or more observers. We believe that the rediscovery of the individuals/ components of the system has given us more points of view from which we can understand the family and organize our practice. We no longer consider the family only as a whole, but we can also cut out from it new systems, continuing until the boundaries of the system are the boundaries of the individual. In other words, we can consider the family as a simple unit, but we can also consider it as a composite unit. In the first case, we are dealing with an observation at a global level: the family exists as a whole, its components fade away as its global properties emerge. In the second case, we are dealing with a local observation: the family is a unit in which one can distinguish components that are endowed with properties that become clear in the dynamics of their interrelations as well as in their relations with the outside world.

Obviously, these two areas of observation are complementary: one does not exclude the other, although we feel that in practice, they do give rise to quite different operations.

Global observation, which emphasizes simple units, seems to us more pertinent to the sphere of theoretical analysis of social systems and of their interactive dynamics (the study of macrosystems, the study of relations between the family and institutions, and so forth). As we pass from the sphere of analysis to that of interaction, we have to move toward localized observation, because, of course, the interaction does not take place with the system but rather with its parts. Therefore, this sphere of observation seems more suited to the therapeutic context, not merely to that of individual therapy, which is quite obvious, but also to that of family therapy. The reader can find examples of this in the clinical cases described in the sections on the present and the future.

A brief illustration of a case of complex interaction between a family and various institutional systems should clarify what we mean by global observation of simple units.

> This case concerns a family that was sent to us by the Welfare Agency because of the learning difficulties and behavioral problems of the youngest child, 7-year-old Laura. Although this family said that they agreed with the advice of the social worker and the educational staff, they appeared very reluctant to have anything to do with therapy. All of the members of the family were present, but they were quite annoyed at having been summoned. They were very thorough in answering the therapist's questions, but were careful not to deviate from the script that they seemed to have learned by heart. They showed the kind of behavior that we have, understandably, found in families sent for compulsory consultations. It was as if they were saying, "We're here only because of the judge's power to make us come, so let's get this over with as soon as possible!" However, in this case, we had no evidence of any court order forcing them to come to our center.
>
> It became clear from the investigation of the referral that many other more important and more powerful systems revolved around this system. This observation allowed us to understand why the family arrived at our Center precisely at that time and, above all, why they had that unmistakable attitude. We saw a relational tangle in which the jurisdictions of various social agencies as well as that of the educational staff, were superimposed. It was likewise apparent how the lines of communication between the systems were broken at many points. The messages seemed to circulate only among the various institutions (however not always); most of the time, they touched the family only tangentially.
>
> This superabundance of professional workers, some of them activated by the family itself, was justified by the system's extremely precarious economic and structural

situation. The father did not have a regular job, and he had been in prison for three years for various misdemeanors. Some years before, the two sons from the father's first marriage had been committed to a reformatory and afterwards put in foster care. The present wife was illiterate. The two children born of this second marriage were not problem-free either: the firstborn was considered disabled because of mental deficiency, and the second child, Laura, the identified patient, had behavioral and scholastic problems.

The history of this family had prompted the educational staff to consider Laura's problems as an indication of parental neglect. These hypotheses, which had their roots in the fertile soil of social stereotypes, were hardened into certainties when Laura told the teacher that her parents permitted her to do whatever she wanted to do, even though occasionally her father would hit her. The school promptly made a report of suspected abuse to the police and to the Juvenile Court. It goes without saying that nobody thought it was necessary to corroborate the girl's statements or to call the parents in for a talk to ascertain the truth of the matter.

The social agencies that were involved in this family's long history had rarely exchanged information, each acting sectorially, limiting its actions to its particular jurisdiction: granting a subsidy, institutionalizing the boys, giving assistance to the family, checking up on the adequacy of parental care, and so forth.

The pathology of the communication among the various systems had transformed this family from a disadvantaged one, which certainly did need assistance, into an abusive family.

Chapter 3 | **APPLICATION OF FAMILY THERAPY**

FAMILY THERAPY AND GENERAL PSYCHOPATHOLOGY

The hospital environment in which we have always worked has been of great advantage by making it possible for us to do therapy with families of the most diverse types of circumstances and pathology. Because this hospital is a public clinic, it furnishes us with a caseload that is quite complete in terms of the range of psychopathology. It has a regular influx of new cases, as well as a constant turnover.

Starting from the beginning of our work here, we have avoided, for the most part, making decisions about the selection of cases. We usually limit ourselves to seeing the families in the order in which they contact us.

Our clinical experience has furnished research material and documentation that have allowed us to individuate parameters that distinguish between the various pathologies with which we have dealt. Even though initially, during a phase that we would call pioneeristic, it seemed to us that we could utilize family therapy for all cases, from psychosis to anorexia, from depression to social psychopathology, without making any distinctions, as our clinical work progressed, we were gradually forced to make distinctions. We will discuss these criteria for differentiating further on.

We continued seeing all of the families that contacted us, at least for the diagnostic consultation phase. In the first few years of our work, we would make a decision at the end of the consultation phase about whether to take on the family for therapy, which at that time would be limited to family therapy. At present, we also evaluate what kind of therapy would be most appropriate. Thus, in our work, we have never made distinctions or used selective criteria for choosing from the applications for therapy. We are always flexible in giving precedence to particularly urgent situations, for example, in cases of anorexia at an advanced stage of physical deterioration.

We have always been against giving precedence for selection, not only for practical reasons (a public institution is by definition nonselective and nondiscriminatory), but also for reasons that have to do with our theoretical principles. We feel that if the sample being studied is heterogeneous, it permits us to draw more reliable conclusions about clinical practice, independently of whether the observations are to be used for a formal scientific study. In fact, we have always applied ourselves to testing the validity of family therapy in general, and, in particular, that of our clinical model. It is impossible for us to separate our roles as researchers from our roles as therapists. In fact, we consider ourselves to be both clinicians and researchers. From our point of view, one must not neglect performing an assessment of the results and a systematic study of the possible areas of application while doing therapy.

In certain periods, it is true, we have have spent a good part of our time dealing with specific types of psychopathology, for example, psychosis and anorexia; however, this had to do with an increased number of applications in these areas from our clients. The increased incidence of anorexia in our caseload has become very noticeable in the past few years. At the present time, it is the disorder that we most frequently treat. This has permitted us to gather a vast amount of observational data that are potentially usable for a research project. In fact, the hospital environment offers the advantage of variety of cases from which one can choose a research project, according to a particular need or a specific interest. Obviously, such a project could not be identical with the clinical activity of our Center, which simultaneously has to satisfy all of the other requests, according to our usual way of handling cases. At the present time, various research projects are in progress, and one is already finished. The latter is a study, carried out in the second half of the eighties, of twenty cases of primary infantile autism, which we will now describe briefly.

FAMILY THERAPY AND AUTISM

In March 1980, the family of a 13-year-old boy who had been in individual therapy for 7 years, asked for a consultation. At that time, infantile autism was, for our staff, an area with which we had not yet dealt; this was the first case we had come across. Full of the enthusiasm and optimism that had characterized our initial approach in family therapy, we had no doubts about obtaining a positive outcome by using the same model for systems with autistic patients.

Something happened, however, in the first consultation session that forced us to reconsider the suitability of the use of family therapy in cases of autism, and, more generally, the advisability of using family consultation instead of the actual therapy sessions. The moment the session began, the patient started showing an acute anxiety that led to violent acting-out behavior: he screamed and hurled himself onto the floor. We cut short the session, having gathered from the boy's behavior signs of his rejection of this therapeutic context, which we thought he might have felt as conflicting with his individual therapy — something he did not intend to forsake.

This episode, which might seem banal at first, caused us to give much thought to two kinds of problems. The first has to do with the advisability of family therapy when therapeutic treatment, albeit of different kind, is already going on. In particular, if the patient already has his/her therapist for individual therapy, is it correct to involve him/her in a consultation together with the other members of the family? Is individual therapy compatible with family therapy? If so, in which circumstances? We will deal with these problems in the following chapters.

The second type of problem concerns the particular type of disorder that we had begun to treat. Is family therapy indicated for autism? Could it possibly take the place of individual therapy for the patient or could it complement individual therapy? We had decided to work out these problems because applications for therapy by families with autistic children were on the rise. We dealt with twenty cases of primary infantile autism, diagnosed within the first 3 years of life, in conformity with the criteria of *DSM-III-R* for autistic disorder.

When health professionals deal with patients labeled autistic, the first problem they encounter is that of the correctness of the diagnosis. Too often the term autism is used loosely. On the other hand, in too many cases, the disorders of early childhood are underestimated, and the opportunity for an early diagnosis, which is absolutely indispensable for effective treatment of the patient, is lost. When we speak of effective treatment we refer to two possible paths, which, however, do not preclude each other. In fact, they can complement each other to good advantage: vitamin therapy (vitamin B6, magnesium, and vitamin B complex) and intensive educational therapy.

What we have noted in these two types of treatment is in agreement with the conclusions of more authoritative specialized studies. In particular, with regard to vitamin therapy, we refer to the data compiled from the completed and returned diagnostic checklists, Form E-3, prepared by the Institute for Child Behavior Research of San Diego, California, directed by Bernard Rimland (1986). Our assessments of the effectiveness of educational therapy for autistic children are based on table 2 of the above-mentioned checklist and on the basic studies of Lovaas (1987) on the results of behavioral modification treatment. In our experience with autistic children, apart from the pharmacological treatment and intensive hyperstimulation of the patient, we do not see sufficiently dependable alternatives, although we do acknowledge that other kinds of treatment, such as holding therapy based on the relational model, certainly have some validity (Prekop 1984, Zappella 1987).

We think that autism is the only type of psychosis that is a syndrome with a genetic etiology, in which the appearance of the symptom cannot be ascribed to the mode of family organization. Although we, as systemic professionals, tend to attribute the origins of the individual's pathological condition to the system to which he/she belongs, in analyzing the communication patterns and organization of the family system of autistic children, we cannot accept the linear model adopted by some other authors, such as Kanner and Bettelheim, who consider autistic behavior to be the child's response to maternal inadequacy, lack of affection, and communicational deficits.

If we begin with these assumptions, it is evident that in diagnosing a child as autistic, one designates the family as well with the child's symptom, implying that the family is autistogenic (whereas we feel that it is, instead, the child's autistic behavior that forces the family to modify its system's organization). This process is the antithesis of what usually characterizes other pathological conditions, psychoses in particular, in which it is the patient who becomes symptomatic in relationship to the family organization.

Another consideration is the persistence of the pathological condition in these cases, which, by necessity, causes the family to seek a stabler, more livable situation, without attempting to resolve the underlying problem.

Our intervention, then, could not be thought of as therapy aiming for change in the family's patterns of communication, but rather as support for the family in order to help it manage the problem and to hold down the high level of anxiety that is always associated with the implicit designation of the system as autistogenic, as well as to redefine the family as being within the normal range. In fact, this is the tendency that emerges, at one level or another, for all of the families that we have seen during the consultation phase.

The objective of our work took form in the preparation of an intervention with the following objectives: the achievement of an acceptance of the disorder on the part of the family, the lowering of the family's anxiety level, and the attainment, on the part of the system's members, of an improved capacity for management of the patient.

Our work plan was thus divided into two distinct phases: a diagnostic phase and one that could be called therapeutic in the sense described above. The diagnostic phase was made up of three specific parts: the filling out of a checklist by the parents (Rimland Test), the compilation of a rating scale about the child by the therapist ("The Childhood Autism Rating Scale" of E. Schopler), and a diagnostic family consultation session, for which a structured interview had been put together. This interview concerned particular areas to be investigated: the behavioral problems of the autistic child as well as the organizational and intercommunicative aspects of the system with regard to the child's autistic condition and the family members' relationship with the patient. Only when we had finished carrying out these prerequisite steps did we make a decision about whether to take on the family for therapeutic consultation sessions.

We saw twenty families for the diagnostic phase, and took on four of them, without the autistic child, for a series of consultation sessions with the above-mentioned objectives. Twelve families were not taken on for consultation sessions because they had demonstrated an adequate level of acceptance of the problem as well as a low level of anxiety. Diagnostic investigation of the four remaining families did not indicate autism. As for the autistic children, those who did not already have adequate treatment were referred to various specialized centers.

FAMILY THERAPY AND ORGANIC SYNDROME

Family therapy is also utilized for systems in which there is a member with an organic syndrome. Various syndromes are so serious that they inevitably trigger significant retroactions in relationships among family members. The object of treatment is not that of curing the organic condition but rather that of correcting various dysfunctional aspects of communication and of relationships in the family.

We would like to illustrate a family therapy intervention in a rather anomalous case: a case of psychological disturbance with serious alimentary complications in a man with Down's syndrome.

The patient was a 24-year-old man named Marco, whose case showed serious organic involvement, and who was later diagnosed with anorexia nervosa.

This diagnosis was made during the last of a series of hospitalizations. The prognosis was inauspicious: death within a month. The hospital records from the first interview, released 2 months prior to the interview with us, presented the following clinical profile: Eisenmenger's cardiopathy, atrophy of one kidney, a history of gastric disturbances and intestinal hemorrhages.

The recommendation of family therapy had been made by the family doctor, to whom the family had turned for advice after the young man had been discharged from the hospital by the staff doctors who said that they were not capable of dealing with a case of anorexia nervosa. Family therapy would have been a last-ditch effort in a situation that offered no alternative solution. However, neither the family doctor nor the family had much faith in it.

During the previous 6 months, the patient had vomited persistently, and as of a few weeks before he came to us, he was no longer capable of eating any solid food. As of the last few days prior to the first consultation session, he was no longer able to hold down the two liters of milk a day that by that time was his only source of nourishment. He also had persistent intestinal hemorrhaging and his weight was now 36 kilograms (79 pounds), down from his normal weight of 52 kilograms (about 115 pounds).

The patient was the thirdborn of four siblings. The two elder sisters, one of whom was married, lived in Germany. The family had lived there for many years, due to a work transfer of the father, a high-level executive in a precision instruments firm. Upon the retirement of the father 2 years previously, the parents and their two sons had moved back to Italy.

Luke, the younger of the two brothers, was in his last year of high school. Marco was enrolled in a social-educational center (S.E.C.), which, however, he had never attended regularly, due to his very poor health. At any rate, this was the reason given by the family for his irregular attendance. Even the workers of S.E.C. were alarmed at the progressive deterioration in Marco's health. As a result, they were hesitant about putting him either in a learning program or in recreational activities. The patient was so debilitated that one could not consider any concrete proposal, even of any part-time activity, at that time.

The first consultation was entirely dedicated to formulating a diagnosis and understanding what the family hoped to achieve with family therapy. The therapeutic team had already formulated two opposite hypotheses in the presession phase.

The first hypothesis was that the symptomatology could be attributed to the pathological symptoms associated with Down's syndrome becoming more acute, in particular, the preexisting gastric disturbances, as indicated by the patient's clinical records. If that were the case, the stress that the parents put on the alimentary problems could have been the understandable reaction to the need to deny the handicap, together with all of the other effects of Down's syndrome, that had progressively affected the young man. In this way, the alimentary symptoms permitted the parents to direct their attention away from the end result of a one-way process, which was directly connected with the patient's Down's syndrome. Therefore, the worsening of Marco's organic pathological condition would have been denied and the responsibility for the current physical problems would have been attributed to an external cause. (This would have been consistent with the diagnosis of anorexia nervosa.) Therefore, we faced a dilemma: should we refuse to deal with a desperate case, explaining to the parents that their son's illness was already in a terminal stage and that it was not a psychological illness? Or should we accept the case, but for a disease that Marco did not have?

The alternate hypothesis was that the patient was expressing his psychological distress in a way that involved the alimentary sphere, although this was not completely consistent with the clinical profile of anorexia nervosa. If that were the case, the concern of the family about the alimentary problems and their request to us to deal with the psychological aspect of Marco's condition would not have been a denial of the gravity of his organic condition. Nonetheless, although the parents had already accepted the possibility of their son's death of natural causes, due to the spontaneous evolution of Down's syndrome, they could not tolerate the idea that their son could die of starvation. Therefore, they requested therapy to remove the psychological disturbance, which was putting the patient at risk for a type of death that could not have been anticipated by Marco's clinical history. The family could not come to terms with death caused by a psychological disturbance, since this was not an inevitable consequence of Marco's organic condition. If this were the case, there was an indication for psychotherapy, but the therapeutic team was unsure of the likelihood of attaining its goals. Would the terrible physical condition of the patient have permitted him to participate actively in the sessions and to draw any benefit from them? Or were the therapists overestimating their capabilities as therapists, such that they could no longer objectively evaluate the situation?

At the conclusion of the evaluation phase, the team was split into these two camps. However, both sides agreed that they had a deontological imperative to act, no matter which hypothesis turned out to be the correct one. It was therefore necessary to evaluate whether to take on the family in therapy, starting from its explicit request for an intervention with the single purpose of resolving the alimentary disturbance, since no attempt had as yet been undertaken. Without exception, the entire team was in agreement that the outlook was not an optimistic one because of the degeneration of the patient's health. However, we felt the obligation not to abandon the family to be deontologically binding, taking precedence over any other consideration. The intervention of the therapists could turn out to be ineffective from the point of view of helping Marco, but it would be fundamental as support for the family in that difficult stage. Therefore, after a long discussion, the team decided to take on the family in therapy. We told them that we would see them again in a month to begin therapy, with the purpose of resolving the eating problem. The therapeutic team told the family that they were optimistic, even though the therapy might require a long time. In this manner, an implicit message was given to the family, almost a dare. Marco was obliged to survive in order to have therapy.

The identified patient arrived at the first session of therapy showing an extraordinary physical improvement. The clinical tests done in the meantime also indicated this change. Marco had begun to eat again and he no longer had any intestinal hemorrhaging, although the vomiting and a series of food-connected rituals persisted.

As the session progressed, the hypothesis that the family would not tolerate the appearance of psychological pathology to put Marco's life at risk appeared more and more valid. The mother, speaking for herself as well as for the others, said that the family could accept the death of Marco because of organic causes, but not "because Marco would no longer eat . . . ."

This second session was clearly the crucial one, in which it became plain that there was a communication disturbance that the therapists connected with the appearance of the symptom. Marco's parents reported their discomfort with his constant, insistent questioning about his differentness (which he very clearly perceived) and his urgent, pressing questions about his getting married, doing military service, and getting a driver's license. These questions, associated with normal events in the life cycle of a healthy young man of Marco's age, created an almost paralyzing anxiety in the other members of his familiy, and stimulated them to search for all sorts of ways to answer Marco without hurting his feelings. They had always avoided stating explicitly to Marco the real reasons that his wishes could not be realized, using instead different pretexts, such as his being too young or his cardiopathy. When he persisted in his questioning, his parents often sent him to specialists to have them answer his questions. Marco, who had a fair amount of self-knowledge, and who was by no means profoundly retarded, had accepted the logic of their answers. However, this maneuver did not work well; there was something about it that did not satisfy him. During the last few months, Marco had given his family no respite from his questions. At this point, the age of the young man no longer allowed his family to put off the explanations that he demanded by saying that he was too young.

During the session, the therapeutic team formulated the hypothesis that Marco no longer accepted the reticence of the members of his family and demanded that they, rather than psychologists and educators, elucidate his problems and communicate with him in an unequivocal manner. Both Marco's parents and his brother, perhaps for the first time ever in his presence, stated that they did not feel capable of answering his questions for fear of hurting Marco. They preferred to leave the task of communicating openly with him to the professionals in the field.

Marco expressed such interest, concentration, and emotional involvement in the proceedings of the entire session that the therapeutic team was convinced of the importance to him of the problem that had been identified: it was the first time that the members of Marco's family had ever spoken of his handicap in his presence, albeit with the mediation of the therapist.

The sons were not included in the second part of the session. The therapist discussed with the parents the problem of communication with Marco, who constantly provoked his family because he wanted clear answers once and for all from them. The parents' distress and reticence were understandable, but it was necessary for them to deal with Marco in a clear, nonevasive manner.

At the end of the session, they were given an assignment that they were to continue carrying out until the time of the next appointment 3 months later. Both of the parents were to carefully observe Marco's behavior, writing down his questions. Each of them was also to write down the answers and explanations that the other gave to Marco, and afterwards they were to discuss them together. In order to maintain the generational boundaries, the therapist told them that they could decide to keep this assignment a secret from their sons or else they could speak about it, but if they decided to speak about it, they were to speak with both of their sons. The parents accepted this, and the sons were asked to come back into the therapy room. The session was concluded in the presence of the youngsters. The therapist said that the parents had been given an educational assignment, which the parents could tell them about if they felt it would be useful to do so.

After the summer, when the family returned for the third session, the parents stated that they had not been able to carry out their assignment (which had not been communicated to the sons), because "Marco had suddenly stopped asking questions."

Marco's physical condition was satisfactory. There was a very noticeable improvement, also indicated in his medical records: a gain of 3 kilograms (about 6½ pounds), practically normal alimentation, and only sporadic vomiting. Marco had regained his normal good spirits and showed interest in everyday activities.

The rapid remission of the symptom, over and beyond our most optimistic hopes, finally permitted the therapists to deal with the dysfunctional aspects connected with the organization of the family system.

Although Marco's situation was one of severe organic involvement, his mental deficit was only moderate. This allowed him to participate successfully in the activities offered by the social-educational center. However, since Marco had not attended the Center regularly, the professional staff had not yet had the opportunity for sufficient observation of Marco to permit them to prepare an individual program suited to his abilities. The permissive attitude of the parents with regard to attendance, while understandable in terms of their concern for Marco's health, showed the effect of the pervasive ambiguity that was characteristic of this family system's communication style. This ambiguity concerned the problem of the handicap. On one hand, it was recognized (Marco went to a center for the handicapped), but on the other hand, it was also denied (Marco did not attend regularly). In other-words, the parents tended not to recognize the problems that were related to Marco's handicap, and therefore they had difficulty speaking about them in an explicit manner. Because they did not require Marco to apply himself to the utmost of his abilities, they ended up treating him in a disqualifying manner and keeping him in a state of dependence such as might be expected of a person much less intelligent.

The therapists' next step was to require Marco to attend the Center daily and stay until two o'clock in the after-noon, although they recognized the difficulties that might occur in putting this into practice. (At this time a longer daily attendance was not possible because of problems that had to do with the restructuring of the Center.)

The fourth session, 2 months later, showed a situation that was already stabilized with regard to the clinical profile. The family had followed the prescription and Marco had regularly attended the Center without compromising his good health. The parents reported that the teachers were quite satisfied with the patient's active participation.

Marco's refusal to eat lunch at the Center was the one remaining problem. An inquiry into the cause of this behavior turned up no pathological elements. Marco simply preferred to eat at home with his brother, secure in the knowledge that his every wish concerning food would be granted. The teachers and the parents preferred not to take a rigid position on this because they were still worried about the eating problem.

It was also revealed that the family and the Center's workers had not discussed together a strategy to eliminate the new difficulties that Marco's behavior presented at mealtime at the Center. The eating problems that the Center and Marco's parents perceived as the cause of the patient's behavior were, instead, the consequence of the ambiguous and contradictory behavior of Marco's two systems—family and Center. The enhanced clarity of intrafamily communication, induced by the ongoing therapy, had brought about a definite improvement in Marco's psychological and physical condition, but there were still dysfunctional communicative patterns in the supersystem made up of family and social-educational center workers, which Marco used to his advantage.

There were also differences in the points of view of the two parents over the possibility of Marco eating lunch at the Center. The father, while sharing his wife's worry about their son's health, preferred that Marco eat with his schoolmates, whereas the mother, although recognizing the value of the group meal as a socialization experience and as an opportunity for learning to abide by a set of rules, preferred to be able to check up personally on her son's eating. The two different positions, the father's, which gave precedence to the rational solution, and the mother's, which had more to do with the dictates of the emotions, were expressed as an ambiguous communication.

At the end of the fourth session, a new assignment was given: it was a test that was justified as a rigorous means of collecting data, which would be then used to decide the optimal solution for the patient. The therapists asked Marco to eat lunch at the Center every day for 2 weeks and then to eat lunch at home every day for the next 2 weeks. The cycle was to be repeated until the next appointment. If Marco were to refuse to eat at the Center during the period in which he was expected to take his meal there, he was not to be allowed to eat lunch when he returned home. Luke was given the daily task of recording the level of anxiety of both parents, using a score from 1 to 10.

At the fifth session, 3 months later, the family seemed visibly satisfied with the result obtained, and that the test had been performed in a precise manner. The prescribed periodic alternation satisfied the patient, the family, and the teachers. Marco was enjoying good health and had applied himself to doing his lunchtime assignment.

On the basis of the father's comment that the lunch arrangements were satisfactory to both Marco and the parents, the therapists proposed an adjustment in the ratio of home lunches to school lunches (70 percent to 30 percent), and released the family from the test prescription, inviting them to discuss this with the teachers in order to agree on a more flexible criterion that would lead to a mutually satisfactory solution.

The last intervention of the team, before dimissing the family from therapy, concerned the evidence of rather high, though not excessive, levels of anxiety, which Luke recorded with meticulous precision. The therapist told the family that if they subsequently felt the need for help in containing their level of anxiety, they could ask for support therapy.

At the follow-up session, exactly a year after the conclusion of the therapy, Marco appeared to be in good health. His only problem had been a bout with influenza that winter, which had left him temporarily debilitated. His weight had stabilized at 50 kilograms (approximately 110 pounds). There was still occasional vomiting, probably due to the gastric problems from which he had suffered for years, as shown by the clinical files from the time before the onset of the alimentary problems.

Marco had been attending the S.E.C. regularly on a full-time basis for several months. He was considered the Center's most diligent and promising candidate, with a view to entering into a work situation. He no longer asked his parents questions about his differentness and they continued to communicate in a more clear and functional manner.

However, the therapists perceived that the family felt a need for reassurance about the stability of the remission of the symptom. The parents reported various food rituals (for example, all serving platters had to be put on the table at the beginning of the meal) that they felt might be signs of a possible relapse. The therapists confirmed that as far as the psychological aspect of eating problems was concerned, the prognosis was worry free. They did, however, explain that the reality of some of Marco's behavioral problems could not be eliminated, since they were due to his handicap, which, by that time, the parents had come to accept.

Part 2 | **THE PRESENT**

Chapter 4 | OUR STORY

THE MODEL IN EVOLUTION

In the course of its history, the field of family therapy has undergone many profound changes. While theoretical conceptualization and clinical practice are necessarily interrelated, they have not evolved together at the same pace. Indeed, much to the consternation of family therapists, there have been phases in which intervention techniques, derived from a paradigm of control from a first-order cybernetics point of view, showed no connection at all with the new directions that theory, influenced by the epistemology of complexity, was taking (Bocchi and Ceruti 1985).

We, too, had been disturbed by this lack of connection but have overcome this uneasiness by working to resolve the problem. We no longer think of ourselves as family therapists, as we did at first. In our opinion, this is a reductive label that does not adequately describe our intervention techniques. In fact, our clinical model has become progressively more and more complex, to the point of bringing us think of the therapy that we do as *systemic psychotherapy*, thus opening up the possibility of working not only with families but also with individuals, integrating specific, diversified interventions. We will justify these assertions in the chapters that follow. For the time being, we will simply state that in the course of the past few years we have made considerable changes in our way of doing therapy. This evolution has come about due to our research work, and it has been punctuated by periods of reflection, doubt, rethinking, and precious intuition. We started out by thinking in a linear, causal style and have moved along a course in various stages, arriving at a systemic and complex mode. We look upon this path as developmental stages of a continuous process. In elaborating a theoretical model to validate and give meaning to clinical applications, the starting point for us, as for all systemic theoreticians in the initial stages of their work as therapists, was the general system theory and the theory of cybernetic models, from von Neumann's point of view. We started out by using paradigmatic models typical of heteronomous systems such as deterministic computers to describe the ways of functioning and the organization of family systems. Systems of this kind use an input–output logic of the black box type, which allows for perfect prediction of the outcome. Accordingly, the therapist, as an external observer, would assess the state of the system and determine its evolution by means of instructive interactions that would tend to bring the system of the here and now toward the desired state of affairs. The use and application of techniques and methodologies that corresponded to this theoretical conception was expressed in a complete and rigorous way in the Milan School model (Burbatti and Formenti 1988).

For about a decade, the Milan Approach was the clinical method with which we identified. We adhered faithfully to this model, not allowing ourselves to be led off the track by other experiences in the therapeutic field reported in the late 1970s and early 1980s. Since our objective was to safeguard the rigor and scientific nature of our premises, we feared that experimentation that did not have adequate controls might undermine this aim. Our temporary withdrawal from the influences in the field allowed us to apply our theoretical model in our clinical practice in a coherent way, so that we could verify the results of our clinical work in a more reliable manner. On the other hand, many of our colleagues shared with us the feeling that there was a need for a rigorous formulation of theory that could serve as the basis for our clinical activity and that could explain it. One must not forget that the family therapy field had its roots in the crisis brought about by criticism of the psycho-analytic model, which has always been accused of a lack of scientific criteria. Therefore, in the first phase of our clinical activity, there were no contradictions, nor was there a lack of coherence between theory and practice.

A rigid adherence to strategies and techniques developed by the Milan School, that is, hypothesizing, circular questioning, and neutrality (Selvini Palazzoli et al. 1980a), guaranteed unconditional faithfulness to the theoretical premises. This first phase of our therapeutic work, which was based on first-order cybernetics, lasted until the early 1980s. However, in the last few years we have been influenced by evolution in the fields of cybernetics, theory of information, biology, and the physical sciences. We have gradually focused our attention away from deterministic, heteronomous systems, with an input–output (von Neumann 1958) type of functioning, to operationally closed, self-referential, autonomous systems (Wiener 1965). The acknowledgment of the autonomy of living systems and of social systems played an important part in the change in the way the role of the observer was viewed (Morin 1986, von Foerster 1981). The implications of the epistemological revolution produced by the new theories of knowledge and by the theory of complexity also had a great influence on us (Bocchi and Ceruti 1985). We passed from the conception of an external observer, able to determine the behavior and changes of an observed system through his/her function of control, to the idea of an observer in structural coupling (Maturana and Varela 1985) with the observed system.

The influences this change of orientation had on our thera-peutic work were quite important, and we will discuss them further on. The coming to the forefront of second-order cyber-netics and the epistemology of complexity in the last decade had brought about a conceptual and theoretical revolution, and it was impossible to remain uninfluenced by it, especially because we, as family therapists, could not avoid this perturbation.

The second, intermediate, phase of our evolution was marked by the formation of a multidisciplinary staff, whose research work has already been described in the first section of this book. We felt then and remain convinced that having a group of people with specific abilities in different areas would allow us to pursue our study of systems from a wider point of view, incorporating the different conceptual models and individual methodologies of the various fields we represented. We felt that it was necessary to integrate different, complementary approaches to the same problem in order to be able to describe adequately a complex object of study, such as a living system or a social system.

This collaborative work certainly enlarged our individual conceptual ranges. Our multidisciplinary group compared models and developed hypotheses in various areas. In short, our group came up with ideas that rapidly changed our mind-set as therapists. However, it seemed to us that there was no parallel evolution in our clinical work, in our strategies and techniques. This was the phase of confusion that we mentioned before, in which it seemed to us that the gap between theory and practice was constantly getting wider and wider. Our theoretical premises had changed, generating doubts and critical reflections on our way of doing therapy; however, the results of our therapeutic work indicated that the clinical model was still valid. We felt a pressing need to close the gap between the changed theoretical orientation and therapeutic practice; it was thus imperative to invent a new clinical model that was consistent with the premises of second-order cybernetics. A smaller research group was organized to deal with this project. We soon realized that the development of a therapeutic model could not be based on an *a priori* decision, adapting strategies and techniques, no matter how innovative and original, to fit into the theoretical framework. The risk in going that route was of constructing a model that was consistent with the premises, valid in the abstract, but with little connection to our experience and our therapeutic work.

Stimulated by the necessity to resolve this thorny problem, we arrived at the third phase of the process that we have been describing. Utilizing an intuition which, as often happens, probably arose from a sense of angry impotence, we began to analyze our work in a systematic manner in order to emerge from this impasse. We looked at the interactions between the therapist and the family, between the supervisor and the therapist, as well as the interactions in the system formed by supervisor, therapist, and family. The construction of a common reality during the course of therapy was the other focus of our interest. Thanks to this *a posteriori* evaluation, we became aware that, in fact, our clinical model had been evolving for quite some time, and that this evolution was expressed by changes in techniques and strategies, as well as in theoretical premises. In the next few chapters we will examine in detail the salient aspects of this evolution, which range from the changes in the roles of the conductor and the supervisor of the therapeutic session to a different utilization of therapeutic tools.

So, transformations were already in the making even before our investigation of our activity, although we were not aware of that at the time. These transformations were certainly connected with a change in our mind-sets as therapists.

Our clinical model had appeared to be immutable, but in reality it had undergone a transformation. To our regret, we were no longer orthodox Milan Approach therapists, even though our change had been so gradual as to become apparent only after a careful study was carried out.

Another element of the result of our study made an impression on us: the point-by-point analysis and criticism of the various aspects of our clinical practice (techniques, strategies, the role of the therapist) brought about epistemological reflections and observations that very clearly effected a change in our theoretical premises. It was evidently a self-referential spiral process, in which theory and practice became intertwined. As one would undergo transformations, it would generate transformations in the other, and vice versa. This is the type of process that the French epistemologists call *bouclages* (Livet 1983).

We finally feel able to describe a clinical model both with the theoretical concepts derived from our *a posteriori* analysis of our clinical practice and with our present conceptualizations. We have proceeded by induction, arriving at general laws and explicative schemes on the basis of data from our clinical practice. Now we are able to explain the conclusions of our work of clinical reflection, illustrating the different technical aspects and the methodology of the model.

A COMPARISON OF STRATEGIES AND TECHNIQUES

We will now illustrate two clinical cases: the first patient was treated using the methodology of the Milan Approach, the second was treated with the techniques of the model in development at that time. We hope that the comparison will clarify the differences of the interventions utilized even if only sketchily. We will examine the technical aspects in detail in Chapters 5 and 6 of this section.

CASE 1: AN ADOLESCENT IN CRISIS

A 57-year-old retired Air Force colonel contacted us to request family therapy for the problems of his 16-year-old son Johnny, who was described as introverted, apathetic, and socially isolated. He was attending a not very prestigious regional vocational institute, in which there were a good number of handicapped pupils with varying degrees of learning difficulties. His class was made up of youngsters who all had some degree of mental deficiency. The reason given for his enrollment in this course was that during the years of compulsory education, Johnny had been a very poor student. According to the parents, their son's scholastic inadequacies were due, in part, to Johnny's lack of diligence, but mostly due to the incompetence of his teachers. The youngster's intellectual capacities, as indicated by his achievement on the Wechsler, were in the range of normal.

The boy's mother, who was 12 years younger than her husband, had married him when he had already been widowed for 4 years and already had a 3-year-old daughter, who had been living with the paternal grandparents from the time of her mother's death. Felicia was the daughter of the second marriage; at the time therapy was begun, she was 22 years old, had been married for 2 years, and had a son just a few months old. Paula, the daughter of the first marriage, was 27 years old, married, and had a 3-year-old son. Both of the young women lived in the same town in Tuscany, having married two cousins. The father, mother, and brother lived in Milan. The father, after retiring from the Air Force, had begun working as a traveling salesman for a pharmaceutical company. He took advantage of business trips to go to see his daughters, to whom he was very attached.

The relationship between the wife and Paula had always been a difficult one, even when Paula was a small child. In fact, Paula had never been taken into the father's new family, much to his regret. All the same, he agreed with his wife that his daughter Paula was quite headstrong. While reconstructing the story of their marriage, it came out that, even though this couple appeared to be close and hid their conflicts well, this basic issue had entrenched the partners in two irreconcilable positions. The hypothesis formulated by the staff was that the wife had always made an issue of her husband's unequal treatment of the two daughters. Even the man's visits to his daughters during business trips provoked arguments between husband and wife. The wife accused her husband of invariably going first to Paula's house and always visiting Felicia last.

However, even though the conflict between the two of them seemed irremediable and had weighed heavily on their relationship for many years, they were, to all appearances, united and incapable of arguing; even Johnny agreed that this was so. The myth of the happy family was certainly valid for this system! (Ferreira 1963).

Nevertheless, whenever the conversation touched on the two sisters, Johnny became very reticent, which confirmed that this was a very delicate subject. As a matter of fact, throughout his life his parents were focused on the two daughters, and in the competition that arose from this concentration they had neglected their son, who seemed not to count for anything at all. Perhaps Johnny had hoped that, after his sisters were married, he could win a place in the hearts of his parents, but little by little, he realized that nothing had changed; even though his sisters were no longer physically present, the competition went on, to his disadvantage. This fact could have accounted for the onset of the symptom, that is, his learning difficulties.

The parents were prompted to action because the school had brought Johnny's situation to the attention of the psychoeducational staff, which had summoned them and, after a couple of sessions, had sent the family to our Center for consultation.

During the first session, the patient was unreceptive, apathetic, and extremely reluctant to talk. He was stimulated to open up partially only by the provocations of the therapist, who tried to get him to state explicitly the resentment he felt toward his parents and his irritation about being brought to our Center. As a matter of fact, this decision was made by his parents without his agreement, and thus he had come determined to hold back his cooperation. With some amount of difficulty, the youngster managed to state that he was very angry with them, but without giving the reasons for his anger. The staff decided to reread his behavior, giving it a positive interpretation: Johnny surely had good reasons for not wanting to tell his parents why he was angry. We explained that probably he was afraid to hurt them, deeming them not strong enough to be able to stand the possible unpleasantness of it. Therefore silence was prescribed for Johnny for the rest of the session, at the end of which only the parents were reconvoked for the second consultation session.

Subsequently, the parents were taken on into therapy, through the maneuver of telling them that the therapists felt that the reasons Johnny was irritated with them could probably be attributed to their son's idea that the parents were focused on something that they considered more important than him. Since their family seemed to be such a close one, in which harmony and mutual understanding reigned, the staff proposed to the parents a series of sessions in order to try to understand, together, how it was that Johnny had come to have such a strange idea, which, to top it off, he was even afraid to reveal.

Therefore, work was begun with the parents, and the label of patient was removed from the youngster, who was never again seen by the therapists. The therapy was done in a somewhat underhanded way, disguised as sessions held to figure out how an adolescent boy had come to certain conclusions about his relationship with his parents. This made it possible to deal successfully with the couple's real problem in ten sessions. Within a few months, Johnny showed a remarkable improvement: he had switched to another school, he had joined a gym, and he had begun to see his teenaged friends again.

In the case that we have briefly summarized above, therapy was carried out on just the two parents, with the identified patient being completely excluded by the therapists. Nonetheless, the restructuring of the subsystem of the two parents had also retroacted on the relationship between the parents and their son.

In the following case, on the other hand, in addition to the therapy conducted with the parents, contact was maintained with the identified patient, albeit from afar, utilizing an intervention modality that is not very orthodox from the point of view of the Milan Approach, which provides for a total suspension of the relationship with any member that is dismissed from therapy at the end of the consultation phase.

CASE 2: THERAPY DONE FROM AFAR

During the first consultation session with a family of four (father, mother, and two children), it became quite clear that Mara, the 14-year-old identified patient, had absolutely no intention of participating in the session that had been requested by her parents.

As a matter of fact, her parents had been quite worried by her recent and unexpected decision to stop going to the high school she had just barely begun attending, and above all they were upset about her very noticeable change of character: she had gone from being a cheerful and happy-go-lucky young girl to a closed and depressed one who was becoming more and more bad tempered with them.

Once Mara had finished giving her personal data to the therapist, she entrenched herself behind a wall of silence, interrupted now and then by spells of crying whenever her parents would attempt to make her talk. The staff, however, was able to understand the meaning of her behavior, and they commented on it and openly expressed their approval of it in front of the parents.

In fact, Mara had decided to come to the Center with her parents but to withhold her cooperation. Her parents were aware of this because Mara had told them in advance, but they were circumspect, at first, about telling this to the therapists.

This decision by their daughter, which the parents read as nasty and spiteful toward them, was really coherent behavior that was quite in keeping with a teenager who felt betrayed by the person whom she had believed to be a true-dealing confidante. This person was a friend of the family, a former teacher, to whom she had confided her scholastic difficulties and her lack of personal conviction in following the course of study that her mother had preferred but that she herself did not find much to her liking. The teacher had, in fact, without saying anything to Mara, advised the parents to request a family therapy consultation session for help in resolving Mara's difficulties.

The therapists, rereading Mara's behavior for the family, expressed support for Mara with regard to her indignation and urged her to refrain from talking.

We planned to take on just the parents, who overreacted when dealing with their daughter's problems, the result of which was an amplification of Mara's distress and the elicitating of reactive behavior on Mara's part. It was decided that Mara be released from the therapeutic context (reasoning that it was a lost cause, since for her it was perceived as her parents' territory), and stressed that any confidante she chose (in that period, Mara confided in a cousin who was slightly older than she), whether friend, adult, or therapist, be strictly hers alone, and that there be no interference by other people.

During the first phase of therapy, the parents tried everything possible to invalidate the decision of the therapists to deal only with the subsystem of the two parents. The most flagrant maneuver was that of bringing their niece (at that time, Mara's confidante) to the sessions, both physically and by way of various letters written by this niece. The therapists refused all of these intrusions, defining firmly, once again, the boundaries of the system with which they intended to deal.

During the course of the therapy, communications from Mara began to arrive, brought by the parents, who had been prevailed upon to deliver a series of messages. After ascertaining that these were not divisive maneuvers on the part of the couple (that phase had already been overcome some time previously and the couple was properly engaged in therapy, in the sense that they had accepted the rules set by the therapist), but rather, authentic appeals of the youngster, we wondered how to respond. In any case, this was an interference with the therapeutic plan, and we must not overlook the fact that this interference was made by a family member who, voluntarily, had been excluded from the therapeutic context by the therapists. On the other hand, the staff felt quite certain that they could consider Mara's messages as authentic appeals for help.

From the parents' reports of Mara's behavior during the previous few weeks, it was clear that Mara was experiencing another betrayal. In particular, she was beginning to sense that her cousin was double-dealing, reporting her secrets to her parents. It was this fact that, on occasion, caused Mara to talk to her cousin, in rather grotesque terms, about her intentions with regard to a life-style incompatible with her family's ethical standards (being a prostitute, a vagabond, and so forth). The parents, having been promptly informed by their niece, were extremely alarmed, thus proving that they had fallen into the trap of the provocations of Mara, to whom they dared not say anything for fear of being discovered.

It seemed to us that Mara felt quite confused, caught between the choice of exposing her cousin, and thus losing the one person who helped her, and that of continuing to confide in an untrustworthy person. Perhaps Mara was contemplating a third possibility: she could bypass her confidante, who by this time was her parents' ally, thus provoking both her cousin and her parents in a reactive manner, and could, at the same time, test the possibility of establishing a relationship with new individuals (the therapists). We read the messages that Mara had sent us via her parents in this sense, as requests to return to the therapeutic sessions.

Since, at that time, we were imbued with the spirit of change and had a revived interest in the family's own reality, we tended toward giving Mara an answer. Even though it was not our practice to exchange messages with absent family members, we felt that it was advisable to take advantage of Mara's communication and thus to open up to her a therapeutic channel, albeit at a distance. Reconvocating her to the family therapy sessions was out of the question, since it would have invalidated everything that the therapists had said and done up to that time.

The path that led to the construction of a therapeutic relationship at a distance was opened by a letter addressed to Mara. The aim of the therapists was to give Mara a means by which she could get herself out of the stalemate in which she found herself at the moment. Among the possible alternatives were the following: establish the conditions for being able to trust her cousin, choose a new confidante, or start individual therapy.

Since the therapists could not verify their hypotheses with Mara present at a therapeutic session, the content of the letter was purposely cryptic. This channel, which turned out to be very useful and was used several times, permitted us to do real therapeutic work with a family member who had, at first, been excluded (though, now we could say, excluded only in physical terms) from the system to be observed and treated. We want to stress the fact that all of the letters given to the parents were sealed in an envelope, so that it would be clear, both to Mara and to her parents, exactly who the people concerned in the relationship in this channel of communication were, and so that the confused circumstances of communication of the past (the relationships with the former teacher) and of the present (the relationships with the cousin) would not be duplicated.

Here is the text of the first letter sent to Mara:

Dear Mara,

During today's session, your parents told us of the proposal you had made to them, that is, that of you and Laura [her cousin] coming to our therapy session.

As you remember, at the end of the consultation session that you attended we said that we thought that if you felt the need to discuss your problems with somebody, it was absolutely indispensable that this person discuss them with you and you alone. It seems to us that you have chosen Laura.

If you feel that you have established a good relationship with Laura, one that involves only you and her, then we cannot grant your request, precisely out of respect for your choice and to avoid interfering with your relationship. In other words, any intervention of ours would be incompatible with what Laura is doing at the moment.

However, if this is not your choice, and you have other proposals to make to us, we would be happy to take them into consideration and discuss them with you.

In the meantime, we will continue to work with your parents, in order to help them hold down their anxiety level.

Sincerely yours,
(the therapists)

Right now, as we are writing about this case, the family's therapy is in its final phase; we have just seen them and set up the next appointment, which we presume will be the last one, for a time 5 months from now. The parents have confirmed that, during the past few months, their daughter has been maturing and has become more autonomous. The relationship between parents and daughter has gotten much better; in addition, Mara is busy and is doing volunteer work for social and humanitarian agencies. Finally, after 2 years of standstill, she has resolved her problem about school. She has become aware of her own needs and now has the courage to rebel against her mother's expectations: in fact, she now attends the school that she had wanted to attend after having completed the course of compulsory education, and which she had, at the time, given up, because of pressure from her mother.

Chapter 5 | **THE REVISION OF BASIC PRINCIPLES**

We feel that it is useful to indicate various theoretical premises before explaining in depth the various aspects of the therapeutic process. Thus, we intend to justify from a practical standpoint not only our current epistemological point of view but also the utilization of our techniques. We feel the need to state clearly our position in the debate with regard to the epistemology of knowledge: what do we know and how do we come to know? We feel personally involved in these questions, since we are systemic therapists who want to acquire more knowledge about the systems with which we find ourselves interacting. Although we are not philosophers, we do intend to state clearly where we stand with regard to a theory of the observer.

Scientists no longer have the illusion that there is an absolute reality, which is objectively quantifiable, as the basis for the phenomena that we observe. The theories of relativity and quantum mechanics have already demonstrated that, even in the world of inanimate objects, the observer modifies reality by the mere fact of observing it. Moreover, the observer actively intervenes when he or she measures and describes objects and events, and thus in a certain way determines or "creates" them.

The image of the scientific observer who, standing apart from the phenomena, objectively observes and describes them has been relegated to myth (Pagels 1982).

Every description is subjective: the object cannot be separated from the subject who observes it. Therefore, were it not for the existence of a consensual domain among various different observers, established *a priori*, in which theoretical premises, language, techniques, and instruments of observation were shared, one could not communicate any description. Moreover, if the object of our study is a living system, instead of a mechanical, chemical, or physical system, then the interactive aspect of the process of observation (in which subject and object together cocreate a shared reality) becomes even more evident. This idea of a *codefinition*, which we share with other authors (Varela 1979), frees us from the dilemma of having to choose between two alternatives that, at first, seem to be mutually exclusive, that is, the epistemology of the representation or the epistemology of the construction. We will not dwell on this problem because scholars more expert than we have already written extensively on this subject.

Our opinion is that both alternatives are equally unacceptable. We have based our theory of knowledge on Maturana's premise that essentially knowledge is action (Maturana and Varela 1985). It is in this sense that we call it a *construction*. Because the object of our study is in the domain of systemic therapy, that object also becomes the subject in an interactive process with the therapist. In this process, the two systems that are concerned (therapist plus family or therapist plus individual) are reciprocally involved in the construction of common meanings. We feel that the best word to describe the result of these interactions is *coconstruction*.

Even though our theoretical orientation has changed, we find that, in our professional language, we are still constantly using terms that seem to pertain to obsolete conceptual models. Although our frame of reference is no longer the representation of reality, we often use words such as *description* or *map*, almost as if there really were a territory to represent. The fact is that to communicate to others that which we are observing, we are forced to describe and therefore to speak or use some sort of symbolic system that we share with the other observers that in some way represents the ongoing interactive process. When we use the term map, we mean to refer to a symbolic, and therefore communicable, description, a contribution to the common construction of knowledge. However, for us, map embodies hypotheses, suppositions, the elaboration of explicative schemes, and so on, that we do not claim as representations of any reality.

In the past we used this term in a different manner, for example, when we were searching for models that would adequately illustrate the functioning of living and social systems. These models, taken from cybernetics, biology, and mathematics, which we studied during the course of our theoretical research, were conceived of as more or less approximative maps, representing a territory that we were trying to approach on the basis of explicative and technical schemes adapted from other disciplines and scientific in nature. We were under the illusion that, in this way, we would get to know this territory better.

This was a course that we abandoned some time ago. We would not deny that it was an important step to take even though it induced us to make an epistemological mistake, which we finally recognized *a posteriori*.

When, in the 1980s, we applied ourselves to the study of the autopoietic biological model of Maturana and Varela, we ingenuously fell into a trap. We utilized this model in the framework of the representation that both we and the authors refuted. The contradiction is evident, for our use of this model presupposed an object of study, that is, the living system or the family system that was separated from the observer, who applied a descriptive model that was utilized in a not very metaphoric sense. The idea that a social system could be considered autopoietic fascinated us for quite some time and stimulated us to continue our research from the point where the authors had concluded theirs. We followed this course until it became clear to us that autopoiesis is a type of organization that pertains to first- and second-order living systems. The autonomy of social systems does not involve the network of biological processes that are necessary for survival—that are reproduced in a cell or in an individual—but, instead, pertains to the capacity for auto-organization in a nonorganic sphere.

The conception of the process of knowing as a codefinition in a consensual domain and as the creation of shared meanings has certain pragmatic consequences. The therapist can no longer be considered to be outside of the observed system but, instead, interacts with it and is thus fully involved in a relationship with it. For this reason, it does not make sense to use techniques and methods that aim to maintain and consolidate the position of an objective observer. Objectivity, conceived of as the capacity for perceptive and cognitive detachment, is an epistemological and practical absurdity. The process of knowing is an interaction in which the observers help to generate the reality that they are trying to understand.

Therefore, it seems logical to us to have this reality emerge from the current interactive context and from the conversation between the family and the therapist, rather than to prepare, in advance, detached from the context of the family-plus-therapist system, a set of rigid norms for conducting the therapy session that does not take into consideration the autonomy of this system.

This point of view means that we have to change our previous conception of the therapeutic team as having a function of control over the family system. We believe that, during the course of the session, the therapist and the family together create a common map. We will subsequently explain how the supervisor similarly extends this map and contributes to making the descriptions more rich and complex. From this point of view, it no longer makes sense to embark on the therapeutic session with preestablished maps (the systemic staff's hypotheses) (Selvini Palazzoli et al. 1980a).

Thus, we felt it necessary to reexamine the basic principles on which the Milan Approach is founded and to redefine the roles of the therapist and the supervisor. It was by analyzing our therapeutic practice that we became aware that, in spite of our efforts to remain true to our principles, we had changed our ideas about what we had previously firmly believed to be the fundamental principles on which our way of doing therapy was based.

THE FORMULATION OF HYPOTHESES

In the Milan model, the presession was of fundamental importance. This was the time set aside for the elaboration of hypotheses. The staff would formulate a series of hypotheses based on the data from the telephone form. (This is the form that is filled out by the nurse who handles the call when a family member contacts the Center to ask for an appointment.) Although the data are quite limited, the staff could still extract a certain amount of information from them. Thus, the therapist would enter into the session armed with one or more hypotheses. These would either be confirmed or refuted by the evidence that would come out during the course of the session. However, it would often become necessary, during the therapy session, to devise new hypotheses to take new information into account. In any event, already at the beginning of the session, there would be a number of more or less overlapping schemes to apply as explanatory models of the rules of organization and mechanisms of functioning of the system under observation (Burbatti and Formenti 1988).

One problem with the preestablished map is that it does not accommodate the uniqueness of various family systems. Our new orientation, on the other hand, emphasizes the unique characteristics of each family system. We now believe that it is only by interacting with the family system that we can develop hypotheses. For example, if a therapist has identical data about two different systems, the same therapist, interacting with each of them, will elaborate different hypotheses in the two cases. It proves impossible to deal with human or social systems by types and classifications. We find it inconceivable to think of a fixed type of therapeutic intervention for a given type of pathology (Selvini Palazzoli 1986). It is equally impossible to define a distinct boundary between functional and dysfunctional systems or between pathological and healthy or normal families. These types of distinctions have to do with an epistemology that is alien to us. We find these distinctions misleading because they refer to the descriptive categories of an observer who believes them to be attributes of an already-established reality.

As our idea of the autonomy of the family system became more and more firmly set, the time we dedicated to the presession became shorter and shorter. Instead of entering into the therapy session armed with hypotheses already worked out with the supervisor, the therapist moved increasingly in the direction of creating common maps together with the family, and of becoming ever more disposed to accept what the family system brought with them, that is, their vision of the world. This different premise frees the therapist from the trap of presuming to know what is reality. It also frees the therapists from the risk of reification of the team's hypotheses. (Reification, that is, extreme objectification, becomes a danger if we forget that this process exists and thus deceive ourselves into thinking that we are not participating in creating the world of human phenomena.)

We would like to refer to the ideas of P. L. Berger and T. Luckmann, and to direct the reader's attention to a book that, although somewhat dated, contains very modern epistemological ideas (Berger and Luckmann 1966). The authors state that it is due to the process of reification that we perceive the products of human activity as if they were something else, facts of nature or results of cosmic laws, for instance. It is due to reification that people think of experiences as if they were the strange creations of some alien force rather than the products of their own creation, brought about by their own activity. The authors conclude that reification is a modality of consciousness. It is the way in which we objectivize the world of human affairs. As Piaget's studies demonstrate, reification is closely connected with our philogenetic and ontogenetic evolution. This phenomenom is not a kind of cognitive throwback; and it is essential that we be aware of its existence as part of our thinking processes. Fortunately, although we perceive the world in reified terms, we have a hand in creating it.

In the past, we thought of hypotheses as models for the interpretation of reality (Burbatti and Formenti 1988) or as maps which represented parts and characteristics of a territory as perceived by an observer (Bateson 1979). Now, because our underlying premises have undergone a transformation, our use of them seems to be substantially changed. At the present time, we no longer think of hypotheses as possible descriptions on the part of an observer with regard to the patterns and communicative interactions that have been crystalized by time. It is, of course, evident that the therapist enters into a relationship with a family that has a history. And that history, the story of events already past, cannot be changed. A therapist can, however, have a part in influencing how that history is now read and in "repunctuating" it, together with the family. In this way, the already-written story of a family can become a different story for the same system that has experienced that history. Even more important is the fact that it is possible for everybody together to aim for a shared punctuation with regard to the situation of the here and now.

We still believe that the hypotheses that the therapist has formulated are useful for organizing the information that the family brings, and for making differences (in Bateson's sense of the word) come to light. However, these hypotheses must be considered less as temporal or causal explanations of events, or sequences of events, in the history of a family for inferring how that family functions and how it will evolve, and more as a means of promoting a shared punctuation that depends not on the observer-therapist but rather on the interaction of this observer with a particular system. When one elaborates hypotheses, one must keep in mind that the family system contributes actively, applying its premises and descriptive categories to the same phenomena the therapist observes.

It was just this focusing on the preeminence of the interactive processes, here with regard to the elaboration of hypotheses, that stimulated us progressively to shorten the time spent in the presession phase. The formulation of hypotheses, as we now conceive of this process, can no longer be limited to one phase of the therapeutic process. It begins the moment the therapist enters into a relationship with the family, and it continues throughout the evolution of this relationship.

NEUTRALITY

The term *neutrality* sometimes erroneously evokes the picture of an aseptic therapist in the role of an external observer with regard to the interpersonal commmunication that takes place in his/her presence. This is the therapist who interacts with the observed system scrupulously controlling his/her verbal and analogic language, thus keeping himself/herself equidistant from each of the system's members. In practice, this kind of therapist is not desirable. And, in fact, being neutral does not mean refusing to get involved in interaction with the system. That would contradict the theoretical principles that call for active participation in the communal creation of an area of shared meanings whenever two or more systems establish a relationship.

The concept of neutrality refers to the global attitude of the therapist with respect to the totality of the system. Neutrality could be considered the resultant effect of the algebraic sum of all of the interventions of the therapist. These interventions would have a positive or negative sign according to whether they are, broadly speaking, confirmations or rejections with respect to the individual members' communications. For reasons of strategy, the therapist can (in fact, is obliged to) temporarily enter into an alliance with one member, as often occurs with the identified patient, who is in the down position. Afterwards, however, it is necessary to patch up the relationship with all of the other components of the system. These are the elements of the principle of neutrality that we still consider valid, that is, functional in correct therapy technique and consistent with its basic theoretical principles (Burbatti and Formenti 1988).

Among the elements of the traditional idea of neutrality that we have retained, and which we consider of fundamental importance, is that which prescribes abstention from value judgments and respect for the family's worldview. By this we mean the totality of cultural and ethical values and norms to which the family subscribes. The functioning of every social group is regulated by its worldview, which, naturally, is connected to a particular context. The therapist is not called on to judge, but rather to understand and accept even the punctuations which do not form part of his/her value system. We have only briefly mentioned these premises, since they are very well known and widely shared by systemic therapists. While sharing these views, we have modified our thinking with regard to a few other aspects.

Perhaps neutrality is one of the concepts of the orthodox view from which our present view has diverged least. Nonetheless, this is a principle that is sometimes difficult to preserve unchanged, given our current propensity to enter to a greater degree into the relationship with a system and, in particular, with its individual members. By entering into a relationship with the members of the system, the therapist becomes part of a supersystem (therapist–family). By carefully applying therapeutic moves in this supersystem, the therapist is apt to break down the equilibrium that the family had managed to achieve over time with a series of adjustments and thus pave the way to establishing a different kind of equilibrium.

Entering to a greater degree into relationship with each member of the family also means allowing oneself to become involved. The therapist who abandons rigid schemes of therapy is more apt to be flexible and to look for an area of concurrence with the punctuation proposed by the other party, allowing his/her own position to be put in question.

At this juncture we would like to present a few interactional sequences taken from therapeutic sessions. We feel that these sequences demonstrate how the therapist who is not worried about remaining outside of the ongoing interactions is able, freely and in a flexible manner, to ally himself/herself with a member of the system.

The first example deals with couples therapy. This young couple had requested a consultation for sexual problems. For several months they had been at an impasse. The wife had no desire for sexual relations. She said that she was no longer attracted to her husband. For his part, the husband had stopped making advances to his wife. He justified his passive attitude by citing his respect for her.

> **Therapist:** Frederick, listening to your wife, I get the distinct impression that she expects something from you . . . for you to take the initiative . . . to do something concrete. . . . Could this be the case?
>
> **Frederick:** I don't know what to say. I don't understand what I could have done to have provoked my wife's reproaches.
>
> **Therapist:** My feeling is that your wife isn't blaming you for anything that you've done, but rather because you haven't done anything.
>
> (Monica begins to sob silently.)
>
> **Frederick:** What could I have done? Certainly I couldn't have raped her!

Therapist: I don't think that your wife was looking for that. Perhaps she hoped that you would have tried to express tenderness and to demonstrate the desire that you say you feel for her. Maybe words aren't enough for Monica.

(Monica nods and continues to cry silently.)

Later on in the conversation . . .

Monica: Frederick denies the evidence. He just isn't able to see reality . . .

Therapist: Can't or doesn't want to, in your opinion?

Frederick (interrupting, in a rather annoyed tone of voice): This is absurd . . . nonsense!

Therapist: Are we making you angry, Frederick? Try to explain a bit more clearly how you see the situation.

From these interchanges we can see how the therapist (while making sure to reestablish rapport with the member of the couple who, at the moment, is in the down position and thus, on the whole, preserving neutrality) uses more liberally the possibility of allying himself/herself with the other member of the couple. In comparison with what we would consider the traditional attitude characteristic of the Milan Method therapist of several years ago, the therapist more explicitly verbalizes his/her own perceptions and hypotheses. Previously, the conduct of the session followed precise criteria that demanded emotional detachment on the part of the therapist and therefore did not permit any exploration of the emotions and sentiments of the components of the family, or any expression of the therapist's (Selvini Palazzoli et al. 1980a). The therapist was required to be more neutral than neutral! At the present time, we can still describe the therapist as neutral, but certainly not neutral in his or her relationships with the members of the family system.

This orientation is just as evident in our second example. It is also a case of couples therapy. The problem that this couple presented had to do with the wife's jealousy with regard to her husband. This, at times, actually took the form of episodes of delirium. As a result of this, a few months previous to the initial session, the wife had been subjected to a forced psychiatric hospitalization.

Wife (crying): I'm the one who has to pay the penalty in this situation! I was the one who was committed! Yeah, I'm the crazy one!

Therapist: Peter, in fact, right from the beginning your wife has given me the impression of being very hurt and vulnerable, a person whose needs have been disregarded.

Wife: Yes, that's exactly how I feel.

Husband (hesitantly): In fact, perhaps I have, in certain circumstances, not taken into account the fact that she is too sensitive. I might have hurt her. . . .

Therapist: Not *too* sensitive, but *very* sensitive.

Husband: Yes, very sensitive. . . . I didn't mean that it's a defect.

Later on in the conversation . . .

Husband: My wife was offended because in the last session I said that, for all of the time that we've been married, she has been a fixture in my life, and when we got home, she blew her top!

Wife: Yes, all I am is "useful" to him. He knows that I'm there for him, that I take care of his needs, that I keep the house in order. He stays with me out of habit.

Husband: That's not how I meant it.

Therapist: Claudia, why did you interpret your husband's words that way? He probably meant that you are a very important person to him in his emotional life, perhaps the most important one of all, that you are the one fixed thing around which everything else revolves.

Wife: Do you think that's what he meant?

Therapist: I interpreted his words that way, but let's hear what your husband has to say. . . .

It seems to us that when the therapist explicitly takes a position, his/her involvement in the relationship with the two partners of the couple induces more incisive restructurings. This may have to do with the therapist's being less focused on technique; and it is probably for just this reason that he/she is better able to pick up on the emotional subtleties that, we feel, permit him/her to establish a more effective therapeutic relationship.

The utilization, or, to be more precise, the nonutilization of neutrality in individual systemic therapy (in which there are different types of problems to deal with) will be discussed in depth in Chapter 8 of the section on the future.

CIRCULARITY

The purpose of the technique of circular questioning is to go beyond the understanding of events and behavior. It is used to get a handle on the relational aspect of the given system as well as the differences in punctuation (Selvini Palazzoli et al. 1980a). Certainly it is a powerful investigational tool, which, when used properly, allows one to gather information and keep track of different levels in the relational network. Every systemic professional knows that when the therapist puts a question, in circular terms, to a component of the system about the relationship between two other members, he/she obtains, in reply, a definition of that relationship as well as a definition of the relationships that the questioned member has with these two people.

Obviously, this communication is not limited to the verbal channel. On the contrary, the nonverbal expression of the person who is answering is very illuminating, and its analysis by the therapist permits a greater comprehension of the present relationships in the system under observation.

Circular questions make it possible to clarify the diverse punctuations of the various family members, comparing the different individual points of view. There is not just one reality to reproduce, but rather numerous realities to be brought to light. In addition, thanks to the technique of circularity, these realities are revealed in terms of relationships rather than facts.

This mechanism also facilitates the elaboration of hypotheses insofar as it forces the person who responds as well as the therapist who is asking questions to make conjectures, to reexamine assumptions, and to make connections between events.

After having utilized this technique for many years, and continuing to use it for the reasons set out above, we feel that we are ready to hazard a few conclusions. Although we still adhere unconditionally to the principle of circularity, acknowledging it as a powerful investigative tool, we do have some doubts about how optimally to translate this principle into action.

As a matter of fact, we have observed that, while circular questions are useful for gaining an understanding of the kinds of relationships that connect the members of a given system, a too extensive utilization of them carries the risk of imparting a rather artificial atmosphere to the therapeutic session. Obviously, this is not the case for every system, but sometimes it happens that some member of the family has difficulty in following the therapist's rather tortuous path of thinking, and occasionally even becomes irritated, expressing this either by openly stating it or by communicating it in a nonverbal manner. This kind of emotional behavior might also be indicative of an attempt to cover up the problem in question and to throw the questioner, who seems too pressing and too suspicious, off the track, though this is not always the case. At times, we have encountered a sort of disorientation and difficulty in understanding the questions, which the therapist then had to clarify and repeatedly explain, weighing down the atmosphere of the session.

Obviously, we are talking about the classical circular questions that deal with three elements of the system; the other so-called circular questions, which have to do with only two members, are more easily understood. For example, there is a difference between asking a father what the mother thinks about an idea expressed by the son and asking him what he believes his wife thinks about some subject that concerns him.

Nonetheless, even when we work with couples, if the circular questions come too insistently and frequently, they appear to create vicious circles, disturbing both partners, causing them to become less collaborative, and ultimately provoking them to become rigid in their viewpoints. In fact, it has happened occasionally, that the disturbance could be ascribed to the sensation of being the victim of some sort of game of the therapist. Among the comments made were: "Let's not play word games" and "What with all of this roundabout talk, we've gotten off the track" as well as "What's this? Another game?" These remarks, which were quite clearly disqualifying, forced the therapist to take steps to regain control of the situation, stressing the therapeutic setting and the asymmetry of the therapist–family relationship.

It was precisely because we were faced with this consideration that we have become less rigid about the use of circular questioning, while nevertheless continuing to think in circular terms. The principle of circularity has remained firm in our minds, and in that sense we utilize all of the answers and feedback of the system. Paradoxically, this even allows us to restore the use of linear questions, which, due to their directness, clearly have a greater impact when exploring the emotions and sentiments of the various members of the family; this is an area toward which we have been tending lately. As we have already pointed out, neutrality, for us, does not imply an absence of involvement in a personal relationship with the individual members of the family. This relationship can be loaded with emotion, the expression of which necessitates a direct therapist–patient channel. Even though it can be very useful to ask a family member about his ideas regarding the perceptions, suppositions, and ideas of another member, we feel that it is more practical to put the question directly to the person with whom we are concerned when it is a matter of looking into his/her emotions and sentiments. This is even more important when the therapist is aware that he/she has established rapport with the interlocutor. A few years ago this area was absolutely off-limits in family therapy, but the recent restoration of interest in the individual in the systemic model has made it necessary to find new methods of and new tools for exploring these areas.

We thus maintain that it is possible for the therapist to adapt himself/herself flexibly to the specific exigencies of the moment in a therapeutic session. One can, for instance, adopt a circular mode of thinking even when using linear questions should one feel the need to be more incisive with regard to a particular area of investigation.

The utilization of circular questions in individual therapy is discussed separately in Chapter 9 of the section on the future.

Chapter 6 | **THE CLINICAL MODEL**

In order to understand what we are doing professionally, a good game would be to imagine answering this question put by a hypothetical conversation partner: "Who are you?" The answer that comes to mind right away is: "I am a systemic psychotherapist."

However, if our questioner wants more explanation with regard to what makes someone a systemic psychotherapist ("But what do you do?"), matters quickly become more complex.

The shortest and simplest way to respond, and, we must say, the first one that comes to mind, is to describe the fundamental characteristics of our basic model, emphasizing the methodological aspects that distinguish it from other models. Afterwards, one could describe the persons who, through their particular behaviors, which we call symptoms, create a need for our role and our task, and thus also our professional identity.

We might conclude by illustrating the kind of relationship that is established between these persons (our patients) and us. It is a very intense relationship. In some ways it is similar to that which is established or has been established with the significant others of their affective–relational world. It is a relationship that in certain ways is similar to that which is established between two friends, between two lovers, or between parent and child, but which also has very specific differences.

Perhaps this answer would satisfy the hypothetical questioner. However, it is more probable that it would perpetually stimulate more curiosity and more questions.

We should note that, in answering, we have paradoxically avoided including ourselves in the analysis of what we are and of what we do. In fact, the utility of the game that we have described lies in forcing us to think about how our actions mark us as therapists rather than as wives/husbands, mothers/fathers, daughters/sons, sisters/brothers, and so forth. We have to go back to our basic principles, the prime movers of our actions.

We are certain that there is no exact, or exhaustive, answer to the question "Who are you?" It seems to us that to comprehend what we are doing professionally we must start by understanding what we mean by psychotherapy; only then can what we do and who we are as a consequence become clear. This game is even more useful if we want to understand and explain what path we have traveled, and, most important, what point we have reached at the present time.

For us psychotherapy is, first of all, an *entering into a relationship with*. We not only enter into a relationship with individuals or groups, but also with a potentially infinite multiplicity of worlds made up of ideas, concepts, myths, beliefs, traditions, and so forth. We enter into a relationship with the sensations, emotions, and feelings of affection of the person who is talking and also with our own, which are the effects of the relationship that we are establishing. We even enter into a relationship with the hypotheses of the colleagues who participate, from behind the one-way mirror, in the development of the therapy.

Psychotherapy, finally, is *entering into a relationship with somebody/something else* in order to construct a reality that did not exist before, in the sense that it is devoid of meaning before it is created by the therapeutic session.

From our point of view, it is, therefore, of little importance, in this phase, according to which basic model one enters into a relationship with someone. Whether it be as an indulgent or strict parent, as a brother, as an inflexible teacher, as a companion, what is crucial is the necessity not only to discover but also to invent, by creating it, a reality with which to work.

We maintain that the steps that we take in the context of our clinical practice are never random but closely connected to more or less structured, theoretical networks, which are certainly analyzable. We like to describe a psychotherapist as, broadly speaking, a scientist whose clinical activity is his/her area of research and the focus of his/her production of ideas. Practice and theory are thus in our scheme bound together in an autoreferential loop in a continuously active process: theory organizes our practice and contextualizes it, while our practice organizes the theoretical premises, in turn, stimulating their development (Morin 1977).

In this chapter, we will deal with the clinical model that is presently being used by our staff, highlighting our evolution from scientists/discoverers of the laws of the world (as ontologically real) to scientists who create reality while interacting with it. We must continue to reflect upon cognition, or, to be more precise, about how one comes to know (that vast and complex subject that has spurred philosophical thought since ancient times). Therefore, we will try to analyze the methodological and technical aspects of our work, making an effort to link them to the theories on which they are based, with the intention of providing the reader an explanatory key to the principles that have always been our guide, and that are the starting point for any new developments.

TWO ROLES IN THE SYSTEMIC THERAPY STAFF

THE THERAPIST

The idea that a biological system, an individual, or a family could not be "programmed" from outside because of the vast range of possible states and internal changes dependent on its organization forced us psychotherapists to make a significant leap of logic, to change our theoretical thinking. We found that we had to give up the idea, which was certainly epistemolog-ically incorrect if undeniably gratifying, that we brought about the recovery of our patients. It is difficult not to entertain illusions of being the prime mover behind the development, the changes, and the remission of symptoms. We would not say that this leap brought about a "biographical shock," but we have had to recognize that it forced upon us a partial redefini-tion of identity.

Our clinical practice was also forced to undergo change. The therapist, the observer of the family system, of its games, and of the world brought by each of its members, found himself/herself playing a different role.

The guidelines of the Milan Approach led the therapist to be wary of the danger of being forced to become an integral part of the organization of a system that was closely connected to the family system and with which he/she was to relate only in terms of therapy strategy. For example, Selvini Palazzoli re-ferred to a "bomb" being thrown into the family system from outside in a clear reference to an input-output model (Selvini Palazzoli 1980). The objective of the therapist seemed merely to be that of unveiling the well-masked family game, dealing with diverting maneuvers of its components. Therapy came to take on the appearance of a gory battlefield and the therapist that of the skillful strategist! The therapist was obliged to avoid becoming a *de facto* component of the family; he/she was merely a part of a therapeutic system, which was founded on the basis of a contract of purposeful and asymmetrical collab-oration. In this contract a complementary relationship was delineated, in which the family that requested help occupied a one-down position. The control of the relationship and of the developmental progress remained firmly in the hands of the therapist, who defined the rules to safeguard the therapeutic situation. It follows that failure of therapy was often attributed to the therapist's unconscious stepping out of the therapeutic context.

On the other hand, there were therapists who were opposed to the introduction of the principles of second-order cybernetics in clinical practice out of a fear that awareness of the autono-mous functioning of family systems would translate into assigning to the therapist the role of an aloof and passive observer.

We do not share the extreme view of those who maintain that whatever the therapist says or does has absolutely no bearing on the system with which he/she interacts, because each and every system is in continuous interchange with its environment.

In our therapeutic practice, the therapist has become even more active. In the therapy session we do not behave like external observers (neither perturbed nor perturbing) who are merely present at the communicative interchanges and inter-actions of the family. This attitude contradicts the premise that human interaction is not programmable from the outside. To be this sort of therapist would be to fail to take into account the fact that any observer becomes a part of the reality that he/she observes, creating it, shaping it, and, in turn, being created and shaped by it. Reality is always created by means of interaction (von Foerster 1981), and this is even more true in a setting like ours, since we deal with human beings.

The person or family that we are getting to know is also an observer system, and therefore is also the subject in the interaction with the therapist. The two systems involved in the therapeutic process—therapist and family or therapist and individual—create shared meanings. The result of this interac-tion is a codefinition of meanings and, in a more general sense, of reality.

That a system is autonomous does not rule out its inherent permeability to the external world and to the other systems with which it has established a structural coupling. The ob-server and the observed end up as part of the same generative loop.

Up to this point we have remained on the level of theory, but, in practice, what exactly is our new therapeutic role?

To begin with, the Milan Approach family therapist, charac-terized in the past by a studied distance from the family members (adopting neutrality as an ethical imperative as well as a technical necessity), is now much more active in con-ducting the session. He/She is more willing to be involved in an empathetic relationship with the other person, in alliances, in taking sides. While our new way of doing therapy might well be taken for granted by those who habitually utilize their selves in their relationships with their patients (for example, Whitaker), for us it is a new approach.

At the beginning of our clinical activity, we identified with the orthodox principles of the Milan Approach which prescribed, among other things, the utilization of a neutral attitude (as described in the section on neutrality in Chapter 5) in all of the phases of therapy. In our opinion, the Milan Approach is a clinical model that has favored teamwork by a group rather than the activity of the therapist alone. It is particularly in this model that the Batesonian conceptualization of the systemic mind is epitomized by the structure of the Milan Approach team. It is mainly within its confines that the production of ideas and explanatory hypotheses, as well as the planning of therapeutic interventions, takes place, thereby generating a continuous process of reciprocal comparison between the group's members. In other words, the systemic mind is most active whenever the team's therapist and supervisor(s) get together for discussion (during the phases of presession, breaks during the course of the session, and postsession).

We believe that the Milan Approach provides less room than other models of family therapy for the use of the therapist's personal potentialities and possible active maneuvers.

Nowadays, we maintain that it is therapeutically important to utilize the sensations and emotions that the therapist picks up on during the course of interaction with the family. Obviously, we are not talking about the therapist's personal systems of beliefs (the danger would be that of using our own ethical categories), but rather about emotions that emerge from the history that takes shape, in the here and now, through interaction with the family.

In the same way, the sentiments and emotions expressed by the individual family members are no longer bypassed on the grounds that they are not pertinent to an investigation of relationships, as we once believed. With regard to this, as we already mentioned in passing in the last chapter, we have partially resumed the use of linear questions, which are better suited for an investigation of the emotional sphere. Therefore, it follows that the therapist no longer focuses exclusively on pragmatic behaviors and interactions. (With regard to this, we refer to the classical question: "Who did what when . . . ?")

In addition to behaviors, the family's and individual members' vision of the world has become important. By *vision of the world* we mean not only the bases of ideas and of cultural traditions, but also emotions and life experiences, however without psychodynamic interpretation. In this way, fully aware that we are creating a common domain, we enter into the history of the therapeutic conversation, which requires moments of particular empathy with various family members in order to take place. It seems to us that none of this tarnishes the principle of therapeutic neutrality.

Nineteen-year-old Martin came to our Center with his parents for a consultation requested by his mother because of her son's aggressiveness (both physical and verbal) toward her. During the course of the session, the mother's extremely dominating behavior, which greatly limited her son's independence, became evident. The mother was extremely possessive of her son and she meticulously kept tabs on him, with the tacit consent of her husband, who, on one hand, shirked his duty as a father, but on the other, labeled his wife an inadequate mother.

> **Therapist to Martin:** I don't understand how you can stand this situation any longer. Doesn't it bother you to be treated like a little kid by your mother? Have you ever thought of leaving home to live on your own?
>
> **Martin:** Of course it bothers me. My mother is exasperating! But it's not so easy to just decide to pick up and go—there's the problem of money. I'm a student.
>
> **Therapist to the mother:** I'm also surprised that Martin's not even more aggressive with you!
>
> **Mother** (more surprised than irritated): But I'm an anxious type by nature, and I worry. If only he would keep me informed, if only he would telephone me when he's out in order to reassure me. . . .
>
> **Father:** I, too, tell her that sometimes she overdoes it. She makes Martin nervous, and that makes him become aggressive.

> **Therapist:** But you just look on! Why don't you stop your wife from controlling Martin in this way?

This brief excerpt from a therapy session shows a marked use of linear and direct questions. These are probably more effective than circular questions in rendering the conversation between the therapist and the system's members more meaningful and in making an emotional impact. In addition to this, the therapist chooses to make explicit his/her own perceptions and personal worldview, presenting alternative behaviors to the family.

This same style is also present in the second example that we cite. It deals with a session with a couple who applied to us because of a marriage crisis touched off by an extramarital relationship of the husband; the relationship had already been terminated by the time the wife found out about it.

> **Wife to the therapist:** I want an answer! He has to tell me why he did it, what it is that he didn't find satisfactory, why he decided to wipe out fourteen years of marriage!
>
> **Husband to the therapist:** But there's no answer that satisfies her! I'm at my wit's end! My wife has been torturing me for months with demands to give full particulars, and I've described everything, down to the smallest details, but this isn't enough for her. Maybe there just isn't any explanation that would satisfy her. . . .
>
> **Therapist to the wife:** Mrs. Verdi, my impression is that your husband is trying to tell you, among other things, that even before this infidelity, your relationship wasn't working out. At the last session he spoke about dissatisfaction with family life, do you remember?
>
> **Wife to the therapist:** Yes, he was tired because he was working at two jobs, we were deep in debt, and the children were very young. He's always had more trouble than I in bearing hardships . . . , but we were together, we had two splendid children, we loved each other. Why wasn't this enough?
>
> **Husband to his wife:** It wasn't just a question of money!
>
> **Therapist to the wife:** Your husband is saying something very important to you—maybe it's the first time he's putting it

'ay attention to him! I think that by devoting all of your
o the problem of his infidelity, you are keeping yourself
oticing that things between the two of you weren't OK
for quite some time. You would prefer to think that your
ge has been brought to the breaking point by your
nd's affair rather than by marriage problems. This makes
uffer less. I understand that. But it seems to me that if you
t want to come to grief, it is necessary that you take note of
it was already happening to your marriage before this affair,
n if this is a horrible thing to accept! Let's try to understand
y it is so difficult for you to accept this fact, and why it is just
hard for your husband to speak to you about it. Now what
as your husband trying to tell you just a moment ago?

Wife to the therapist: Maybe that he no longer loves me.

Husband to the therapist: It isn't that I don't love her any
longer. I love her more now than before. My wife has always
had her own particular way of loving me—with an almost
suffocating love. I've often thought that it would be better if she
would love me a bit less but understand me a bit more!

In the next example, we will show how the use of a linear
style, almost inductive in some places, permits the therapist to
ally himself with a psychotic patient, making it possible for the
latter to communicate directly his disagreement with his parents to them (in particular to his mother) for the first time since
the onset of his illness, without resorting to clearly pathological
behavior.

This is the case of 24-year-old George, who had already
embarked on a "career" of chronic mental illness. He was
the only child of two people who were forever at odds. In
particular, the choice of school and field of study for their
son, beginning with the choice of a specialized high
school, had been a bone of contention for the couple, who
had begun to send contradictory messages and paradoxical injunctions to their son with regard to this subject.

After a brilliant scholastic career, shadowed only by a
brief episode of mental disturbance (in his third year of
high school, George had been hospitalized for a few days
because he had heard voices), the young man had been
forced to suspend his university studies, which he never

resumed, because of a serious psychotic breakdown, cha
acterized by delirium and hallucinations. George came
us a year and a half after he had been diagnosed as havin
a hallucinatory psychosis, for which he was being treate
with drug therapy.

Therapist to George: I'm absolutely flabbergasted that every
time that you take a bit of time to think of how to answer a
question of mine, either your father or your mother intervenes
to help you. Or, like what happened just a few minutes ago,
your mother says that you are out of contact, that you lose
control of yourself, and so on. It seems to me that they are
treating you like an idiot! Haven't you ever felt that you were
being treated like an idiot by your parents?

George to the therapist: Well, yes, sometimes, by my
father.

Mother to the therapist: Naturally! He says it all the time—
even today, when we were coming here, he said to me, in a loud
voice, "Look at the idiot you've raised!"

Therapist to George: And your mother? Don't you feel that
you are being treated like an idiot by her?

George to the therapist (after a quick glance at his mother): I
couldn't say.

Therapist to George: Earlier, your mother said that you had
difficulty understanding, because you are often out of contact; is
this the first time that you've heard her say these things?

George to the therapist: Expressed in this way, yes, it's the
first time.

Therapist to George: And doesn't this make you mad?

George to the therapist (after glancing at his mother): Yes,
really mad, because she thinks that I'm an idiot!

Therapist to George: You don't seem very angry to me. If I
were in your place, I'd be much angrier! Even my colleagues are
amazed at your calm. When is it that you feel treated like an
idiot by your parents?

George to the therapist: All of the time. But, I've always said,
I've done all that I can do; I can't do any more than that!

Therapist to George: Is this the reason why you hit your
mother? Because you feel really mad at her when you feel
treated like an idiot?

Another basic difference in our way of doing therapy can be seen in the final phase of the session. In the past, this phase concerned the therapist's direct intervention at the end of the session. After having consulted with the supervisor(s), the therapist proceeded to introduce the therapeutic input into the family system. Usually, this would take the form of a paradoxical injunction or a ritualized prescription of homework; in any event, the intervention would be of a prescriptive type (Selvini Palazzoli et al. 1978). Nowadays, the therapist's final intervention is formulated from the substance that has come out in the session, supplementing and extending it, in terms of alternative readings and restructurings. Often, the intervention is created during the entire course of the session, beginning with the "building blocks" brought by the family, that is, from the different punctuations of its members and from their system of beliefs regarding the problems discussed. At the end of the session it is sufficient to repropose an alternative, restructuring reading, which emerges during the interaction, summarizing briefly, but effectively, the essential elements.

At this point, we would like to present a final intervention of the type that we have just attempted to describe.

In this case, the final intervention coincided with a consultation session with a family consisting of two parents and their 16-year-old daughter Bonnie, an only child. The father had applied to us upon the recommendation of the family doctor, a friend of the parents, indicating problems in managing their daughter, who was described as difficult and rebellious. An episode in which Bonnie went out in the evening without their permission and spent the night at her boyfriend's house was described by the parents as "running away from home." After this episode, Bonnie was put under rigid control: she could not go out nor could she use the telephone, and she was no longer allowed to associate with her boyfriend. During the course of the session, it came out that the anxiety for their daughter, while shared by both of the parents, was, however, emphasized by the mother as a means to call her somewhat elusive husband back into the marriage relationship. Certainly there were some problems in the relationship between the parents; however, they did not show any disagreement with regard to their daughter, nor did they argue in her presence.

It was necessary to remove the label of patient from the daughter, who, moreover, did not seem to be suffering, but was merely reacting in a somewhat theatrical manner, more to make a point than from conviction. In fact, she recognized that her parents had the right to exert control over her, but she felt that the punitive measures taken against her were excessive.

We have transcribed in detail the final intervention of the therapist:

Your family doctor did well to suggest a family therapy consultation, because very often in cases similar to yours there are risk factors which can sometimes lead to an unhealthy situation. Some deviant behaviors of teenagers are signs of deep psychological distress and of real suffering, which would be dangerous to ignore.

However, it seems to us that this is not the case in your situation. We feel that, even with all of the problems connected with your daughter going through adolescence, your family has the resources to deal with the various difficulties.

We are aware that the conflictual parent–teenager situation that is typical of adolescence is often a source of discomfort in a family, but we nevertheless feel that we can reassure you that there are no pathological elements. It is normal that your daughter make demands for independence, that she be reactive with regard to her parents, and that she wish to assert her own rights; but it is also just as healthy for parents to expect to exercise their prerogatives as parents, making rules and putting limits on their daughter, after agreeing on what measures to take.

Therefore, the necessary conditions for therapy do not exist; that is, there is no indication for family therapy. If this were not the case, we would have reason to worry. If Bonnie, at 16 years of age, did not demand some space of her own, did not request to go out with her friends, in brief, did not make any demands, then the situation would seem to us quite worrisome. Likewise, if you parents abandoned your role of control, adapted to the age of your daughter, then we would also feel cause for alarm. In that case, we might have advised family therapy.

THE SUPERVISOR

Our conception of the role of the supervisor has undergone a very definite transformation over the last few years. This is a very important node in the network of our reflections, the one that we have discussed the most. Its introduction into a second-order cybernetics model must be reinterpreted, for it is not readily justifiable.

In the Milan Approach, the supervisor's most important function was controlling the interaction between therapist and family and, therefore, the development of the therapy, specifically by overseeing the proper use of therapy tools and techniques on the part of the therapist. (Here we use the term *therapist* in the particular sense of therapy session's conductor.) The supervisor's function of control was only superficially camouflaged by the Batesonian idea of *systemic mind* applied to the therapeutic team (Burbatti and Formenti 1988).

Thus, the supervisor was conceived of as an external observer, at a metalevel, who intervened in the therapeutic process with respect to adherence to the basic principles, of which he/she was the guarantor. There was an assumption of a hierarchy of observation levels, from the inside (therapist) to the outside (supervisor); the supervisor was thus at a higher level.

Consistent with these assumptions, communication by intercom was one-way: the therapist could only listen; he/she could make neither rebuttals nor comments. Nowadays, we no longer recognize the supervisor as being on a metalevel with respect to the system formed by the therapist and the family, that is, he/she no longer has the function of control. The supervisor–therapist–family supersystem becomes an auto-referential system in itself. From an organizational point of view, it is a closed system.

The supervisor has retained the specificity of observation level with respect to the other systems that participate in the therapeutic process. This gives rise to a difference in the type of observations as well as a difference in the resultant descriptions produced by the supervisor with respect to those of the therapist. The levels of observation are, without doubt, different; they differ, however, not in terms of hierarchical order, according to the theory of logical types (Whitehead and Russell 1910–1913).

We would like to suggest the metaphor of a fan in which different, but hierarchically equivalent, perspectives and points of observation converge on a single, observed center. This conception allows us to combine the separate descriptions such that the resultant description is situated at a clearly higher level of complexity. In this way it has become possible to delineate a richer map, by means of the construction of a common reality.

During these last 2 years, as we analyzed the supervisor's interventions, we became aware that the loss of the control function was expressed in technical changes and by a different use of the therapeutic tools, while the setting remained the same. However, we cannot exclude the possibility that sometime in the near or more remote future there may even be changes in things pertaining to the setting. We have in mind the one-way mirror and the intercom in particular.

In the Milan Approach, the function of the one-way mirror was to keep the supervisor in the role of external observer and to protect him/her from the risk of involvement in interaction with the family. At the present time, while we feel that the one-way mirror can be used to maintain specificity in the supervisor's level of observation, we do not exclude the possibility of achieving this purpose by other technical strategies that could work just as well.

The new theoretical guidelines, according to which all observers are considered to be hierarchically equivalent, though occupying different perspectives, imply that the use of the intercom should decline or at least be modified. According to our theoretical principles, it would be more advantageous for the therapist to leave the setting in order to discuss matters or to consult with the supervisor whenever either one considers it advisable to do so.

In order to understand better the process of integration between the work of the therapist and that of the supervisor, we have analyzed as a specific research project the use of the intercom during supervision as provided for in the Milan model. The interventions of the supervisor by means of the intercom that were recorded in the past 2 years were examined with particular care. We compared the communications that had to do with cases that had already been terminated with those that were still going on. Thus, we empirically used a time parameter to differentiate between therapy that was carried out based on first-order cybernetics and therapy that was based on second-order cybernetics.

In comparing the past and present cases, the most apparent changes are: a less frequent use of the intercom and a less directive intervention in the therapist's work. The current interventions are not so much suggestions of what to do and references to orthodoxy as suggestions of hypotheses and alternative punctuations. This is consistent with the recognition of the autonomy of the therapist–family system. In fact, the steps that we take in the context of practice are never random, but are instead strictly connected to theoretical networks, and are analyzable.

From the observations of these videotapes, it appears that the supervisor tends more and more to avoid making direct suggestions or indicating the method to use for analyzing the various topics. He/she limits himself/herself to describing what he/she has observed, organizing the data according to his/her conceptual point of view.

In order to highlight the differences in the intercom communications based on first-order cybernetics and those based on second-order cybernetics, we cite some of the taped interventions selected from those reviewed in the course of our research.

INTERVENTIONS BASED ON FIRST-ORDER CYBERNETICS

Nineteen-year-old Vincent was the only child of a late middle-aged couple. In his last year of high school, he had begun to show symptoms of regression and rejection of social relations. The parents, especially the mother, had invested much time, love, and energy on their son, who, up to that time, had had a promising scholastic career, and they had hoped for a brilliant future for him.

During the session, the mother repeatedly brought up the topic of school.

Communication of the supervisor over the intercom phone: "Ask the father why the son sighed when the mother spoke about his scholastic successes."

A 27-year-old woman had requested a family therapy consultation on account of her anorexic 17-year-old sister. The family was made up of the two daughters, the father, the mother, and a 22-year-old son.

The therapist was looking into the family interactions at mealtimes.

Supervisor: "Ask the brother what the father does at mealtimes when the mother insists that the sister eat."

This case deals with a family composed of a father, a mother, and a 21-year-old son. The husband had requested a consultation because of his wife's depression. Both members of the couple were simple manual laborers, elementary school graduates; in contrast, the son was studying law at the university.

From the beginning of the session on, whenever the father would speak, the son would intervene with disdainful comments about him or else snort with impatience.

Supervisor: "Metacommunicate about the son's disqualifying attitude toward his father. Ask the mother: 'Does your son always speak to your husband in this tone of voice?'"

INTERVENTIONS BASED ON SECOND-ORDER CYBERNETICS

This family (discussed earlier), was made up of a father, a mother, an 11-year-old son, and a 14-year-old daughter, who was the identified patient. They were sent to our Center by a teacher, to whom the daughter had confided her scholastic difficulties and her reluctance to pursue a high school course for which she felt she was not suited.

Afterwards, the teacher spoke with the parents, suggesting a family therapy consultation.

Right from the beginning of the session, the girl seemed apathetic and uncooperative. Whenever the conversation touched on the teacher, she refused to talk.

Supervisor: "It might be that the identified patient feels betrayed by the person who referred the family here and who discussed family therapy only with the parents."

A young, married couple (she was 24, he was 25) had applied to us because of sexual problems. They had been married for almost 4 years and had a 3-and-a-half-year-old daughter with Down's syndrome. They had married at the beginning of the eighth month of pregnancy, and from the very beginning of the marriage, the couple had only had sporadic sexual relations, which were very unsatisfactory. The reason given was a lack of willingness on the part of the wife, who said that she no longer felt attracted to her husband to the point that she was in favor of a separation.

From what they had said, it appeared that the husband was still very much involved in the relationship with the wife, who, on the contrary, rejected him. Nonetheless, the nonverbal communication of the wife appeared to be inconsistent with what she said. She showed emotional involvement, which was in apparent contradiction to her words.

Supervisor: "I have the impression that, even though she talks about separation, the wife is still very much involved in the relationship with her husband and that she uses the subject only to provoke her husband into defining the relationship."

The father of a 16-year-old girl (discussed earlier) had requested an appointment at our Center, indicating difficulties in managing his only child. In the preceding months, she had once left home for the night. The parents described this as running away from home.

During the course of the session, the youngster appeared very reactive with respect to her parents. The conversation started with the rebellious behavior of the daughter, but quickly shifted to the mother's difficulties. The latter was depressed. Notwithstanding an apparent agreement with her husband regarding the daughter's problems, she felt neither adequately appreciated by him nor adequately backed up by him in her treatment of her daughter .

Supervisor: "It occurs to me that maybe there's a tacit alliance between the father and the identified patient. The two of them might have utilized the girl's distress as a pretext for bringing the mother to therapy."

We hope that one can deduce from the interventions that we have briefly related that the supervisor seems now to have the function of producing descriptions of the ongoing therapeutic process. These descriptions, however, are to be integrated with those of the therapist who conducts the sessions.

Therefore, it seems that there is now a process of modulation among the three systems of family plus therapist, supervisor plus therapist, and supervisor plus therapist plus family, that contributes to the creation of explanatory maps, which are useful for analysis of the case and for planning the therapy.

PHASES OF THERAPY COMPARED

We will briefly summarize and compare the various phases of the Milan Approach therapy session, their characteristics and objectives, with those of the current model. We hope that this comparison will make clear the developmental changes that we have tried to describe up to this point.

THE MILAN APPROACH
(FIRST-ORDER CYBERNETICS)

The Milan model therapy session is made up of various distinct, but integrated, phases. Selvini and her co-workers described four phases (Selvini Palazzoli et al. 1978):

1. presession---> staff discussion
2. session---> direct interaction between therapist and family
3. postsession---> staff discussion
4. final intervention---> direct interaction between therapist and family

Actually, this division reflects theory more than practice, but it is possible to find characteristic elements that belong to each phase:

1. *Presession:* The staff analyzes the available data (telephone form, files containing notes on the past session[s]), and it makes hypotheses regarding the family game going on. This phase lays the groundwork for the therapist's entry into the therapy session that is about to start. The staff formulates various alternative hypotheses that are to be tested.

2. *Session:* The therapist gathers information from the family in order to test the various hypotheses that had been formulated by the staff in the presession. At the same time, he/she introduces information into the family system by means of the interview technique (circular questions, metacommunicative observations, alternative punctuations).

3. *Postsession:* The staff analyzes and makes conclusions about the situation, considers both the new information and the hypotheses formulated at the presession, and checks to see if these hypotheses are useful for constructing explanatory maps regarding the family game going on.

If there is to be a final intervention to close this session, it is constructed at this time.

4. *Final intervention:* The therapist, having reentered the therapy room, comments on what has been brought to light by the conversation or prescribes an assignment to be carried out, and then takes leave of the family. Generally, the final intervention is presented in the form of a prescription (ritualized, paradoxical prescription). The therapist never directly communicates what the staff thinks about the case; the communication is structured so that it functions as nonlinear input which is disruptive of the family's patterns of communication (paradoxes, alternative punctuations, and so forth). There is a

constant effort to introduce novel elements as input. Only rarely does the family hear what the team thinks the family expects from them.

5. *The processing of feedback from the family:* This phase occurs outside of the spatial limits of the therapy room (where the therapist–family relationship interaction takes place), but not, however, outside of the limits of the therapeutic context. (This is our addition to Selvini's list.)

The therapeutic conversation—and, even more, the final intervention—functions as input, affecting the structure of the family system. The feedback resulting from the previous session's final intervention is noticeable during the next session, and it will be analyzed by the therapeutic team. Since this has to do with changes that concern the structure of the entire group (the family), it is necessary to give the system a sufficient amount of time for restructuring to be completed. It is for this reason that the sessions are scheduled about a month apart. In some cases, the interval can be as long as 3 months (Selvini Palazzoli 1980).

THE NEW MODEL

We will use the same names to describe the phases of the session of the new model that we used for those described above. Nevertheless, these phases have taken on quite different meanings and functions with respect to those of the Milan Approach. It is possible that, in the future, the ongoing revision of our new model might lead to a more radical change in the character of the session's phases or possibly even to the elimination of some phases.

1. *Pre-session:* This phase has been condensed considerably, both in the case of the first interview of a family (one consultation session) and in the cases of therapy sessions held during the course of treatment.

a. *The first session:* The staff becomes acquainted with the data that the nurse has gathered by phone and entered on the special telephone form.

No hypotheses are formulated about the family game yet, this being deferred to the course of the consultation session—the "reality" is created in that situation, that is, in the interaction. A single, preliminary, very rough hypothesis may possibly be formulated. This will be developed further during the session.

In this phase, the therapists are more concerned with the relationship between the family and the person who indicated family therapy to them than in the nature of the ongoing game. If they formulate any hypotheses, it would be relative to this relationship that they would do so.

b. *Therapy already begun:* The team briefly reviews the case, considering again the various points about the relationship established between the therapist and the family that came out in the preceding session. On the basis of the team's comments, the staff plans which areas to look into or which problems to discuss with the family. It is kind of a warm-up phase, which permits the team to prepare itself for the therapeutic encounter, anticipating a few aspects of the investigation.

2. *Session:* This is the most important phase. It is mainly handled by the therapist who conducts the session since it is felt to be of extreme importance to safeguard the autonomy of the functioning of the therapist–family system. The supervisor intervenes infrequently, and when he/she does intervene, this intervention is interpreted as a description of what the supervisor sees happening in the interaction between the therapist and the family. The supervisor's control function has definitely declined. The number of calls on the intercom has decreased considerably, although they have not entirely disappeared. The calls serve to allow the supervisor to convey his/her descriptions to the therapist so that the descriptions of the team's various members are brought together.

The therapist and the family codefine the history/problem of the family, while the therapist works out his/her own hypotheses on this subject.

The supervisor codefines the history of the therapeutic process—the way he/she sees it develop—through the interaction with the therapist–family system (which he/she observes from behind the one-way mirror), while working out his/her own hypotheses on the subject.

During the session, information is not unidirectionally introduced by the therapist. Rather, the therapist participates with the family in a process of codefinition. The therapist does not only consider the system as a whole, but also pays attention to the individuals who make up the system. The therapist is not only ready to pick up these individuals' relational language, but also looks for communication that deals with emotions and feelings.

3. *Post-session:* The team meets, that is, it unites again as a whole system. The therapist and the supervisor(s) coordinate their observations, thus bringing their different points of view into common focus, and they evaluate the current situation with regard to the progress of the case and the therapy.

Strategies of intervention are planned.

4. *Final intervention:* The therapist reenters the therapy room and concludes the session with the final intervention. Prescriptive interventions are used less and less, since they are in keeping with an idea of control rather than with one of coevolution. Generally, alternative readings and repunctuations are used, keeping in mind that the family system is an autonomous system.

5. *The processing of feedback from the family:* The length of the interval between sessions has remained unchanged, except in the consultation phase (which is now interpreted as a phase of diagnostic evaluation). The two consultation sessions are therefore closer in time (an interval of 1 to 2 weeks).

The interaction between therapist and family is an interactive exchange of considerable importance, which leads to processes of compensatory restructuring in the family (and also in the team). The modality of the family's response is more affected by the organizational and structural configuration of the system itself than by the form of perturbation produced by the therapist. It is always this configuration, in interaction with the environment, that determines the developmental possibilities of the given system, in accordance with the given family's particular rhythm for effecting change.

We feel that the observation and analysis of family restructuring is of extreme importance. They can give us new bits of information for the comprehension of how a given system functions. The more we understand about how a system functions, the closer we get toward unlocking the black box and discovering its works.

Part 3 | **THE FUTURE**

Chapter 7 | FROM FAMILY THERAPY TO SYSTEMIC PSYCHOTHERAPY

During the course of the past 2 years, we have changed our titles from family therapists to systemic psychotherapists. This is not just a simple substitution of a label, but rather a fundamental change in the content and form of our therapeutic activity, which opens up new possibilities in our work for the future.

We intend to justify our change in title to systemic psychotherapists. The motives, which we will now briefly summarize, will be illustrated more fully in the following chapters.

The most important reason behind this change is that the object of our observation and study is no longer only the family taken as a whole unit but also the individual as a system that realizes its autopoiesis within various different social systems (Maturana and Varela 1985).

Many clinical workers have already recovered this area of the individual, resolving an old dispute about the systemic model and the psychoanalytic model. Even though family therapy came into being in open opposition to individual therapy, the controversy seems to have been resolved. In fact, an alternative to analytic individual therapy is emerging more and more clearly, that is, systemic individual therapy, which we will subsequently discuss.

It has appeared more and more evident that in many cases the complementary and/or parallel use of the two treatment techniques (i.e., family therapy and individual therapy) was advisable, while, in other cases, for example, in situations of severe infantile psychosis or eating disorders, individual therapy was the treatment of choice. In general, we have seen that family therapy works mainly in the here and now, when the symptom is still present, or in situations of acute symptomatology that have not yet become chronic. If the patient's distress is connected to problems of the distant past, only individual therapy can allow the individual to relive various fundamental stages. We will discuss in another section the discriminatory criteria that guide us in formulating a therapeutic indication.

Some years ago, systemic therapists proposed family therapy as the panacea for all ills, thus rendering the recommendation of family therapy almost automatic at the end of the consultation phase. Now, however, we tend to evaluate the situation on the basis of various parameters that can be compared (age and personal characteristics of the patient, age at onset of the symptom, chronicity, configuration of the family system, phase of the family's life cycle, etc.) before deciding on what type of referral, if any, to make. Moreover, an indication of individual therapy is practicable even within the systemic relational model, even from a theoretical point of view, since we are still dealing with interactions between systems (although they are special systems, like individuals).

Although it is simple enough to justify the substitution of the word *family* with *systemic* to describe our therapeutic work (in fact, with regard to certain aspects, the reasons are quite obvious), one could not say the same thing for the introduction of the term *psychotherapy* in a context in which any term with the prefix *psycho-* was excluded as a matter of policy. On the other hand, although we recognize that our origins lie in behaviorism and in pragmatism, we have to admit that our present orientation is not only toward behaviors and interactions, but also toward the individuals' emotions and feelings, that is, toward the emotional sphere. We find that we are traveling through a territory that is quite out of the ordinary for systemic therapists, so that it is necessary to proceed cautiously. However, given the present state of our research, we feel that we can no longer ignore any sector of research that reveals itself to be essential to our purposes. With our intervention, we aim not so much at the remission of the symptom (which, naturally, is always to be desired) as at demolishing the premises that are the basis for the family pattern or for the organization of the individual-system. We are not only referring to conceptual premises, but also to the sphere of emotions and meaningful experiences which are a constant point of reference for all individuals. It is on the basis of these, in addition to the interactions in the here and now with other systems, that the relational dynamics, which we observe, are produced. This does not have anything to do with introspective or projective techniques that are utilized in other models, since we do not explore the unconscious, but allows us to maintain our specificity without encroaching on a field out of our area of competence.

Having made these clarifications, which we hope are exhaustive, we would now like to deal with the innovative aspects of our clinical work in general, which have taken the form of systemic psychotherapy. Although these innovations are still in an experimental stage, they open up views of a future that has already to a great extent become a reality.

DIAGNOSIS

The consultation phase in the orthodox Milan model consists of one session, or two sessions a month apart. At the last consultation session, the therapeutic staff gives its conclusions. These initial consultations were supposed to be used for checking whether or not there were indications for family therapy. Nonetheless, most of the families were taken on, since it was felt that this was a model that was applicable to the most dissimilar situations, from serious mental illness to couples conflict or problems of social deviance, such as juvenile maladjustment, and so on.

Since other types of therapy were not considered, the indication of family therapy at the close of the consultation phase had become virtually automatic. It was not considered necessary to change therapists. The consultation phase became, in practice, virtually the first two sessions of therapy. Furthermore, the behavior of the consulting therapist did not differ in substance from the behavior of the same person in the role of conductor of therapy, except with respect to the choice of particular areas of investigation. The consultation period was dedicated to the reconstruction of the family map, including the family of origin of the two parents, and to a detailed analysis of the referral, besides dealing with the nature of the family's request for help and looking into any history of therapy that there might be (Burbatti and Formenti 1988).

The first two sessions were a month apart, just like the therapy sessions that were to follow, as if to reaffirm that the distinction between consultation and therapy was more formal than concrete. In practice, it was a therapeutic context right from the beginning. The family was more or less assumed to be engaged right from the moment a member telephoned to ask for an appointment. It was taken for granted that, by the end of the consultation phase, the family would have accepted the indication of family therapy. Therefore, the family was informed of the date of the first session of therapy without ever being given a chance to decide whether or not to accept therapy. Nonetheless, the family had the last say in the matter, since they were able to decide whether or not they were coming when they were telephoned by the nurse a week before the appointed day. It is significant that the system was not given the chance to decide whether or not to go into therapy and to request it before we set up an appointment. The therapeutic contract was transformed into a one-way indication coming from the therapist.

Our attitude toward the therapeutic contract began to change a few years ago when we started ritualizing the therapeutic contract phase. We no longer take for granted the family's assent to any proposal of therapy we might make. We explicitly request that all of the members discuss it before accepting it and contacting us again. We have introduced a clear break after the phase of consultation to emphasize its specificity and to differentiate it from any successive therapy sessions.

This change answers our own need to characterize the consultation phase as an explorative phase of observation in order to give an indication regarding therapy. We call it a diagnostic phase. In order to avoid any possible misunderstanding, we shall clarify what specifically we mean when we speak of a diagnostic phase and in what sense we use the term *diagnosis*.

From the discussion of our theoretical principles in the preceding chapters, the reader can probably infer our position regarding this subject. Since we do not look at things from a realistic point of view, we cannot conceive of diagnosis as simply the reconstruction of the etiological factors that generated various symptomatic behavior, that is, as an *instructive* diagnosis. This follows from our view that the definition of pathology or normality of a system belongs to a descriptive category of the observer and, thus, is always relative. From our point of view, the consultation phase corresponds to wider objectives than that of merely aiming at drawing a map of the distress and suffering borne by the system, in nosographical terms.

Nonetheless, because we work in the clinical field, we are forced to refer to diagnostic categories that are universally recognized, that is, those of *DSM-III*, which we use for descriptive purposes. However, we do not agree with workers in the field who use these categories in order to carry out preestablished interventions valid for all cases that show similar symptomatology. The practical necessity of being able to communicate to other clinical therapists the results of our observations about the symptomatic areas requires us to classify by typology. Nevertheless, there is not a fixed correspondence between a given diagnostic category on the one hand, and a specific therapeutic indication, or definite, invariable type of intervention on the other.

In this respect, we are quite different from those in the field of clinical medicine, who associate each pathological condition with a specific treatment. This treatment could be either pharmacological or surgical, but it is always measurable and repeatable. In our case, the identification of a particular diagnostic category is not an indispensable prerequisite for doing therapy. What *is* absolutely fundamental is the analysis of the relationships and of the communication between the members of the system that applies for consultation. We have seen that every family has its own particular character, in structural and organizational terms and, moreover, participates in generating, in the interaction with the therapist, the "reality" with which we work. It is still a fundamental objective of the therapist to identify the problems pertinent to the relational dynamics of the system so as to put together a correct proposal for therapy, but that proposal is not automatically applicable to other situations even though they may correspond to the same nosographical category.

Given the change in our basic premises, even the interval of time between the consultation sessions (of which there are usually two) has gradually been shortened. Since it is desirable and often essential to conclude quickly the process of observation and diagnosis in order to formulate an indication of therapy, it is illogical to schedule these sessions far apart.

Nowadays, more and more often the therapist who conducts the session is a different person from the consultation-phase therapist. The therapist who does individual therapy with a member of the system is never a person who works or has worked with that family.

The consultation phase is thus substantially different from what it was and continues to change. Some of our goals have already been realized and we have already seen some of the results of these changes, while still others are planned for the future.

THE INDICATION FOR THERAPY AT THE CONCLUSION OF THE CONSULTATION PHASE

The dilemma of "which kind of therapy to recommend?" is in many cases equivalent to the question of "which system to summon?"

We have already explained that when a member of a given family requests an appointment for family therapy, everybody who lives under the same roof is asked to come, although this system is not necessarily the same one that will later be treated in therapy.

It often happens that therapy or a series of sessions for observation or support is proposed for a subsystem, usually that of the two parents. Very often, the problem that a family brings forward at the consultation session(s) is a child's distress or problematic behavior, meaningfully connected with the parents', although the discord is generally well masked. In such a case, one could decide to dismiss the child in order to continue working exclusively with the parents. For examples, we refer the reader to the first chapter in the section on the present.

In other situations, family therapy could be set up for a subsystem (usually the parents) while concurrent individual therapy could be recommended for the identified patient. We have already mentioned that the consultation phase now leads to diversified interventions. The recommendation can vary. Since family therapy and individual therapy are no longer seen as mutually exclusive alternatives, there are various different combinations within the range of possibilities.

THE THERAPEUTIC RECOMMENDATION AS A CHOICE BETWEEN TWO ALTERNATIVES

Most usually it is the case that preference is given to one of the two alternatives, family therapy or individual therapy, after weighing a series of parameters held to be discriminative for the choice of therapy best suited to both the family and the identified patient.

The age of the identified patient is the first element to consider for the recommendation of therapy, and this is related to a second factor that we consider important: the current stage of the family life cycle (Rodgers 1977). If one is dealing with children up to the beginning of adolescence, their state of emotional and physical dependence inclines us toward family therapy. With the exception of serious childhood psychoses, such as autism, for which there are other factors to be taken into consideration, the symptoms of distress in childhood are always traceable to dysfunctional familial patterns, and for this reason, we tend toward therapy that involves all of the members of the family.

However, for young people from about 18 to 25 years of age, who are becoming independent of the family, the recommendation is most frequently for individual, analytically oriented psychotherapy (of any type). This allows the patient to go through, once again, the basic stages of emotional and cognitive development, reliving past experiences, resolving intrapsychic conflicts, and completing the process of emancipation from the family system. We feel that this kind of treatment is the most suitable for this age range, without regard to the type of pathological condition, except for psychosis.

It has been our experience that for psychotics, family therapy is the treatment of choice, even well after childhood. It goes without saying that psychotic symptoms are closely connected to the dysfunctional patterns of ambiguous and paradoxical communications by the parents in the system of which the patient is a member. However, it is important to note that it is necessary to treat with family therapy when the illness is still in the acute phase. By *acute phase*, we mean within a range of time that is not more than 1 year from the appearance of the symptoms. According to the cases that we have observed, although every case is somewhat different, the effect of chronicity begins to tell about 2 years after the beginning of the symptomatic behavior. In our experience, if the patient's psychotic condition is chronic and the symptoms have already become a firm part of his/her psychological structure and/or he/she cannot be disengaged from the various therapeutic systems without serious repercussions (here we refer to a long history of illness), then family therapy is seldom effective. Naturally, the probability of success decreases in proportion to the time passed since the onset of the illness. We have thus concluded that in cases of long-standing chronicity, the only feasible recourse is pharmacological treatment. Even though it does not resolve the pathological condition, it does keep the situation under control.

"COMPLEX" TREATMENT STRATEGIES

What we have said relative to childhood has some validity also for adolescence. However, we must take into account the fact that the process of emancipation from the family and becoming part of the peer group begins (or ought to begin) in this phase. In cases in which this process is particularly deficient or where there is a serious state of distress and suffering, traceable to the organization of the family and specifically to problematic relationships with basic significant others, we tend toward a more complex recommendation: a referral of the patient to individual psychotherapy (most frequently to analytic psychotherapy) and, at the same time, a series of consultation sessions with the family, which permits dealing with the tensions that are always generated by the presence of a third person in a relationship with the patient. In fact, we are dealing with patients who are still quite young and therefore still very dependent on the family. Therefore, the parents are usually ambivalent with regard to a recommendation for individual therapy or about requesting it for a son or daughter: on the one hand, they accept it or ask for it, and, on the other, they tend to interfere and to contact the individual therapist to be reassured with regard to their own anxieties. Another objective of family therapy in these cases is that of protecting the individual therapy. If the family is not covered, there is the possibility of invalidating the therapeutic relationship of the youngster. Among the pathologies of adolescence, the neuroses are the ones that best lend themselves to individual treatment.

The above-described treatment strategy, which we could call mixed (family therapy plus individual psychotherapy), seems to us especially useful for toning down the stigmatization of the patient, which the recommendation of individual therapy alone runs the risk of emphasizing.

In any event, we feel that individual therapy with the patient cannot be ruled out, especially when, in spite of the youth of the patient, the symptoms have become chronic.

> A typical case, with regard to this point, is that of a 13-year-old girl who had an extremely structured obsessive-compulsive neurosis. The mother had requested a family consultation, seemingly prompted by concern about the condition of the daughter, who involved her to a very great extent in her eating and sleeping rituals.
>
> Right from the first session, it became clear that the mother aimed to bring back into the relationship with her the very elusive father. The girl, whose neurotic behavior began when she was 10 years old, was exploited by the

parents, who, moreover, kept their marriage conflict very well masked. We felt that, since this pathology was already chronicized, couples therapy, no matter how it was carried out, would not have been sufficient to obtain a remission of the girl's symptoms. Instead, concurrent individual therapy was employed, which helped to overcome the situation, setting it on the road toward normality.

Another option that is considered at the end of the consultation phase is the recommendation of family therapy which lays the groundwork for a subsequent recommendation of individual therapy for the patient. We have adopted this type of strategy several times in the cases of young adults, still very dependent upon the family, who expressed a deeply felt need for involving the other members of the system, in particular, the parents, in the therapeutic experience.

In these cases, family therapy makes it possible to deal with the crucial nodes in the relational network, while postponing for subsequent treatment in individual therapy various problematic aspects that are more strictly personal.

A case of this kind involved Tania, a 25-year-old anorexic, who had requested a family consultation at our Center, having chosen between two alternatives proposed as equivalent by the endocrinologist who examined her: individual therapy or family therapy. The young woman had no doubt in her mind, holding that her problem was strictly associated with the family situation, and thus had to be resolved inside the family.

Tania was the second-born child. The 28-year-old brother Max had been married for 4 years, and had a 3-year-old son. Although he lived away from his parents' home, he had maintained close ties with the family of his childhood. He had a special relationship with his mother of which the sister, by her own admission, had always been jealous.

The whole family was in agreement in attributing as the cause of Tania's illness the young woman's impression that she was less loved than her brother. Her parents said that this impression was not founded in reality. The anorexic symptoms had arisen 2 years after Max's wedding, and had been in remission from the time that the parents had agreed to participate in a couple of sessions with a psychologist. (This was before the endocrinologist had stated his conclusions.) With regard to this, Tania had stated that the devotion of her parents and their loving concern had immediately made her feel better. She repeated over and over, like a chorus, that finally, with the initiative of requesting a family consultation, they had set out on "the right road." In this way, Tania made it clear that, in the event of opposition by her parents, the anorexia that was in remission could become acute again. Thus she controlled the situation by holding the power of renewed symptoms over the family.

The hypothesis of the therapists, which was proven to be true during the course of the session, was that Tania had hoped to win back a place in her mother's heart after the marriage of her brother, but had been disappointed: the brother continued to be very much present in the family system, emotionally if not physically. However, from the time when the sister had become symptomatic and ever more intolerant of his presence, Max visited his parents' house less frequently in order to avoid making her condition worse. Thus, Tania seemed to have obtained her objective of ousting her brother from the family. However, the parents stated that they were adapting themselves to the situation only until the reestablishment of normality and expected a return of their son to the system before long. Tania and the parents were, so to speak, wrestling for power: Tania, with her symptom, seemed to have them under her thumb, but, on the other hand, the parents never did completely reassure her.

Had the therapists agreed to the request of family therapy, they would have allied themselves with Tania, reinforcing her power. On the other hand, if they had rejected the request, they would have virtually guaranteed a relapse. For that reason, they resorted to a strategy of recommending a series of observation sessions with the system, in order to keep under control a situation that seemed to be already improving. The proposal of therapy put in these terms could satisfy everybody. In order to counteract the power of the symptom, during the final intervention the therapist told the family that Tania's perception of having been neglected by the mother in favor of the brother was not the cause of the anorexia, as the family had thought.

Actual therapy had been carried out, giving rise to a restructuring of the system, redefining its boundaries with respect to the brother's new family. This outcome has-tened the normalization of Tania's health.

However, in spite of the clear improvement from an organic point of view and the complete recovery of weight, one symptom unaccountably remained: amenor-rhea. As we have often observed in other cases of anorex-ia, the persistent continuation of amenorrhea, despite the restoration of all of the other organic functions, takes on a very precise meaning in the love relationship that the anorexic has with her own partner. In this case, Tania, who had been engaged for 5 years, had stated that she could not marry until she once again felt entirely feminine. Thus, she had a pretext for postponing getting married. A symptom that, in the past, had been connected to the anorexic symptomatology, thus took on a new meaning, which shifted from the sphere of the family to a more personal one as well as to the domain of her couple relationship. For this reason, at the end of the cycle of family sessions, individual therapy was proposed to Ta-nia, and accepted by her, for dealing with some more intimate, personal problems, which were felt to be still unresolved. This individual therapy brought to light fears and second thoughts that she had with respect to her couple relationship and made it possible to surmount the problems. A year after the beginning of therapy, the menstrual cycle was again regular, and Tania had begun to make concrete marriage plans for her future.

In the above-mentioned case, the individual therapy carried out was systemic therapy. According to our criteria, this kind of therapy is the most suitable for adult patients of approximately

25 years of age or older, who generally need an analysis of the situation in the here and now to overcome a relational impasse.

The two strategies of treatment that we have shown above, that is, individual therapy together with family therapy and individual therapy after family therapy, are the ones that we utilize most frequently with adult anorexics. In evaluating the effectiveness of both types of individual therapy, we analyzed the results of the past few years. We believe that systemic therapy and analytic therapy are of equal value. Our experience with anorexia is based on about a hundred cases that we have followed during our clinical activity, 70 percent of them dealing with adults, for whom individual therapy was recommended. About half of this group received systemic therapy and the other half were referred to psychotherapists of other schools. The follow-up, taken at 6 months and at 1 year from the end of therapy, shows percentages of success that are practically equal for the two situations.

For adolescent anorexics, our preferred recommendation remains family therapy. With regard to this, we are in agreement with the authors of the article "An Evaluation of Family Therapy in Anorexia Nervosa and Bulimia Nervosa," which illustrates a comparative study of two different types of treatment, family therapy and individual therapy, the discriminating factors for the choice of therapy (Russell et al. 1987).

THE EVALUATION OF THE "BYPASS"
APPLICATION FOR THERAPY

We would now like briefly to discuss one last point which is of great importance from a practical standpoint. At times, one has to consider a request made by one family member for individual therapy for another member of the system—usually applications made by a parent for a son or daughter. Should one accept such a request? If so, in which cases? What kind of treatment should be proposed? Naturally these questions are more easily answered in the cases in which parents make the request for a minor.

One day a therapist on our staff was informed by our Center's nurse that a woman had telephoned to request individual psychotherapy for her 25-year-old daughter who had sexual problems. What answer to give the woman, who was going to call back in a few hours, had to be decided upon.

Whether it was the case that the young woman (who was, after all, already an adult) had asked her mother to call, or that the mother had herself had taken the initiative to contact the therapist, the fact remained that for such an intimate problem, we would have expected the request for individual therapy to come from the person directly involved, despite the fact that she was still living in the parental home. Thus, it seemed evident that, taking into account the age of the daughter, the maternal intervention revealed a very involved mother–daughter relationship.

Given the lack of independence of the young woman, it seemed that the dysfunctional system was that made up of the mother–daughter dyad (although one could hypothesize that the father, if he was alive and lived with the family, must also have played his part in the family system).

All of these considerations should have led us to favor family therapy instead of individual therapy. Indeed, how could the process of autonomization—which the therapy is—begin if the form of the request for therapy and the subsequent acceptance of the case negated autonomization. Usually this seems to us a good discriminant criterion, although not the only one, for deciding to accept a request for individual therapy: the patient must come to us on his/her own. However, little by little, as our clinical practice progressed in these years, and the sample of patients and their requests proved ever more diverse, it became apparent that even when it came to deciding whom to convocate for therapy, it was not possible to adopt inflexible, unchangeable criteria.

In this case, the therapist who was contacted decided to take on the young woman individually on the basis of the following considerations, subsequently reconstructed and discussed with the therapeutic staff. Even if it were plausible to hypothesize the existence of a dependent relationship between the daughter and the mother, or the parents, it was just as evident that summoning the whole family, justifiable as it might be from the point of view of theory, would have been tantamount to confirming the type of particular structure of the system and perhaps also the family's assumptions that although an individual is grown up, she has to deal with her personal problems inside of the family. We feel that such is the power of context marking of family therapy. We refer here to the Batesonian concept of context marking as a *matrix of meaning* (Bateson 1972) and we have to remember this.

However, there was one aspect of the request on which we could not compromise: the young woman had to arrange the appointment directly with the therapist who had made himself available. Therefore, it was communicated to the mother that her daughter had to telephone personally to get in contact with him.

This counterrequest, which implicitly set up some of the therapeutic rules, still left open to the system and to its components the possibility of deciding which moves to make. The daughter could have telephoned, evading the control of her parents, albeit merely on the basis of a prescription from outside of the family, or else she could have not telephoned, confirming the hypothesized involvement. In this second case, it is probable that another therapist would have been contacted in the same way, but this is conjecture, because it did not happen.

The choice we made seems to us more consistent with our recent theoretical acquisitions. Our hypothesis about the lack of independence of the patient need not translate into a standardized answer: it was necessary to leave open to the system the possibility for alternative moves, consistent with the idea that living systems are in continuous development in relationship to other systems.

The young woman did telephone the therapist and subsequently entered individual therapy, which brought to light that the stated problem was just another pretext, used inside of the family, to avoid becoming independent and differentiating herself from her parents. As long as her sexual problems persisted, she could postpone her marriage to her boyfriend, a person whom her parents did not like.

Thus the hypotheses formulated at the time of the telephone call from the mother turned out to be correct. The mother's initial intervention, however, did not prevent individual therapy from taking place, which made it possible for the daughter to create a protective barrier from parental intrusions. This brought about the resolution of the case in a relatively short time.

The utilization of a sufficiently flexible methodology does not mean a lack of theoretical and practical bases nor does it imply reliance on the therapist's inspiration of the moment in choosing what kind of therapy to recommend any more than on other, purely random factors. We insist that clinical practice be based on a theoretical framework, whose principles serve as a guide for practical applications. However, our recognition of the autonomy of living systems has toned down the rigidity with which we used to apply certain basic schemes. This has given rise to a general procedure of checking, case by case, the usefulness of the basic criteria of the model and also their practicality.

We would like to cite another typical case, in which a flexible attitude on the part of the therapist made it possible for Anna, a 21-year-old bulimic woman, to begin individual therapy. This case illustrates a different initial approach from that of the case described in the preceding example.

One day, the mother of a young woman telephoned the Center, requesting a family consultation for their only child's bulimia. However, she made it clear that her husband was adamantly opposed to participating. The urgency with which she asked for our help and the strongly emotional tone of her verbal communication persuaded us to depart from our usual procedure. (Expressing deep concern for her daughter, she cried and said that she was in despair because of the refusal of her husband to participate in therapy.) Thus, an appointment was set up for a somewhat anomalous consultation, which involved only the mother–daughter dyad.

The objective of this session was to evaluate the possibility of proposing individual therapy for Anna, taking into consideration her age and the refusal of the father to participate, which left no other alternative. However, it was necessary to check to see if the daughter was motivated to have therapy, since the request was not made personally by her. If she was not already motivated, we wanted to see if she could be motivated to enter therapy. This turned out to be easier than expected, even though Anna had a symbiotic relationship with her mother; a single consultation session was sufficient. The following week Anna began therapy. Gradually, both mother and daughter learned to deal with the anxiety generated by the separation initiated by individual therapy. The eating problems were slowly reduced in the space of a year and a half. When therapy had been terminated, Anna, who up to then had been unemployed because of her serious problems, had found a job as an office worker. She was planning a trip abroad during summer vacation with a friend of hers.

Also in this case, the individual therapy that was carried out was systemic therapy, concentrated on relational dynamics and on changing the patient's premises (the so-called restructuring!) (Watzlawick et al. 1974). As we have stated, when dealing with patients of Anna's age, usually our tendency is to indicate analytic psychotherapy, because we think that it is much more fruitful to work at a deep level and on the intrapsychic dynamics. However, in particular situations, we cannot avoid taking into consideration the explicit needs of the patient with regard to the necessity to limit time and cost.

Chapter 8 | **SYSTEMIC COUPLES THERAPY**

This is a chapter on a subject particularly dear to our hearts. It was in the domain of the couple that our rethinking about family therapy had its beginnings. It began to occur to us that couples were uncomfortable in the traditional family therapy setting—or maybe it was we who were uncomfortable, which, after all, is the same thing. Many couples explicitly requested more frequent sessions. We, too, felt the need to shorten the time between our appointments with them. In many cases, the interventions ended up being so weakened by the passage of time as to be less stimulating. Couples seemed to reelaborate the interventions much faster than families did. They also tended to establish a more emotionally involving, individual-type relationship with the therapist. They demanded alliances with the therapist more often and with more urgency than members of larger families normally did.

Thus, we began to modify the setting for and frequency of the sessions, adopting an individual-therapy context for couples. Sometimes this was done after therapy had already begun, but was not yet at an advanced stage. We were surprised at how positive the results were and thus were spurred to develop our thinking about both theory and practice further.

It is our feeling that the couple is more like the individual than any other type of system. The couple seems to manifest needs and problems akin to those of the individual. A family system usually consists of various generational levels (parents, children, and perhaps grandparents). We believe that this characteristic makes the strategy of family therapy obligatory. This strategy also allows for interventions in the subsystem consisting of the couple (i.e., the parents), but it remains family therapy.

Both members of a couple, however, are on the same generational level. This makes an individual-therapy type of context practicable. Often, though, it seems that the partners are not on equal terms—that they are not on the same level—and that there is thus a sort of generation gap. One of the partners may seem to be, or, at any rate, to put himself/herself forward as the parent of the other. But we generally agree with the affirmation of Whitaker (1989) that husband and wife have the same emotional age, that is, that the division of levels is just an illusion.

We have also noticed that, at times, the two members of a couple tend to manifest a similar symptom. Although each expresses his/her own discomfort with a different intensity, both do so through behaviors that, when carefully analyzed, turn out to be comparable. We turn now to a case that illustrates the individual nature of the couple. It is a case that is very meaningful for us because it represented a turning point in our therapeutic work.

A married couple had requested therapy because of the wife's recurrent delusions of persecution. She had been subjected to obligatory medical treatment at which time she had been diagnosed as a borderline psychotic patient.

When, during the presentation of the therapy setting at the beginning of the first session, the therapist mentioned the supervisor behind the one-way mirror and the video-taping of the session, the husband began to show very clear signs of distress and anxiety. He purposely interrupted the therapist's explanations several times before finally explicitly telling the therapist that he was apprehensive about being observed and studied. In spite of the therapist's repeated attempts at reassurance, the man remained distrustful and uncooperative for the remainder of the session. We could not avoid coming to the conclusion that he was more paranoiac than his wife.

This was the first couple for whom we changed (after three sessions) the setup for therapy–weekly sessions in a normal professional office, without contemporaneous supervision. Both husband and wife reacted to the change in a positive manner. The husband even went so far as to say that he felt at ease at the therapy session and felt comfortable about coming to therapy.

Although we often observe a certain homogeneity in the type of pathology of the members of the couple, we have found that more often the two partners communicate their distress through different channels and behaviors and therefore, also, different symptoms. What is clear is that there is no such thing as a couple with one "healthy" member and one "sick" one; instead, there is a common suffering, though it may be expressed in different ways. Each member of the couple reinforces the suffering of the other, and, in turn, is reinforced in his/her own suffering.

At the beginning, our change in the setting for couples therapy was a progressive process and had to do with the circumstances of particular cases. We will cite a few of these cases in this chapter.

We have already mentioned the possibility that the setting for family therapy, which is normally not perceived as particularly anxiety-provoking, can touch off paranoia, as in the case just cited, due to the presence of the one-way mirror and the video recorder. Our experience is that this type of retroaction occurs more often in cases in which the system requesting therapy is a couple rather than a larger family. We do not know whether this correlation has a causal basis or if it is simply random — we have not yet looked into this. We merely mention it as a stimulus for reflection, certainly for ourselves and perhaps as well for others.

It is particularly advisable to reduce the interval between sessions in situations in which there is symmetrical escalation or in which the level of tension and distress is so high as to provoke dangerous episodes of acting out by one or both members of the couple. The danger of losing control of the situation is perceived, sometimes in a particularly dramatic manner, by the couples themselves, who ask us to give them more effective help and to mediate to resolve their conflicts.

> This was the situation of a couple, Julius and Sara, who had applied to us after their relationship had deteriorated greatly due to the wife's jealousy. The husband, who was a federal employee, had had a brief love affair with a co-worker. The affair had already come to an end when the wife began to receive anonymous phone calls relating various details about her husband's extramarital affair. Sara, who attributed these calls to her ex-rival, reacted with obsessive behavior directed against her husband, whom she continuously tormented with questions about the affair (to which the husband, however, seemed to attach very little importance). Julius was irritated to the point that he feared he might lose control of himself. During the couple's frequent fights, in which even their two preadolescent children became involved, Sara and Julius reached the point of verbal and physical violence. To overcome her state of anxiety and depression, Sara took higher and higher doses of psychoactive drugs.
>
> Sara and Julius explicitly asked us to schedule frequent sessions to help them resolve their conflict. They feared for their children's and their own safety, since the tension level was extremely high. The very same request was also put forth by the children, in a very direct manner. In spite of their tender age, they were very much involved, helping their parents by physically separating them whenever their fights passed from words to blows. We perceived their attitude as being that of parents who, after trying everything without getting results, were bringing their two unmanageable children to the specialist. The effect of our accepting the case was that the children were greatly relieved. The parents told us that, since therapy was underway, the children had stopped taking care of their parents' problems.
>
> In this case, couples therapy was decided upon at the end of the two-session family consultation period. The

children were thus freed from the oppressive task of taking care of their parents.

We have used this procedure, that is, a family consultation in a traditional-type setting as a prelude to couples therapy in a changed setting, on many other occasions. We have used this strategy of change of setting even when therapy had already started. One situation which calls for this approach is that in which marital problems come to light after work has already begun with parents of seriously symptomatic children (the children having been referred for individual therapy). Often what is proposed to the parents are sessions for observation, support, or help in containing their anxiety, free of the connotations of therapy, even though, in fact, these are therapy sessions intended to safeguard the child's individual therapy. Below is an example of this type of situation.

This family was composed of a 47-year-old father, a 39-year-old mother, 18-year-old Linda, and 14-year-old Rosie. By the time the father contacted us, Linda had already been anorexic for a year. She had been hospitalized twice and had had forced feedings administered to her during her stays. Linda, who was 1.75 meters (5 feet, 9 inches) tall had reached a low of only 31 kilograms (68 pounds). At the time of the first family consultation session, she weighed 34 kilograms (75 pounds) and appeared extremely exhausted physically. She had an excellent capacity for rationalization as well as a clear perception of her problems.

With regard to her parents, but particularly with regard to her mother, Linda was very reactive. She was sarcastic and cutting in her speech, and she did not spare them from scathing expressions of her opinions. Although she included her father in her criticisms, it was immediately clear to us that her demands and hopes were directed primarily toward her mother. It was mainly her mother that Linda tyrannized. It was her mother whom Linda wanted!

Linda's mother seemed adequate as a mother, apparently emotionally involved in her daughter's problems. However, the more carefully we observed her, the more unaffectionate she seemed. She did not express any emotions or emotional closeness. She seemed to discharge her motherly duties as if they were an unavoidable obligation, and without much maternal feeling.

In spite of Linda's strong dependence on her mother, individual therapy was possible because Linda was quite introspective and because she was moving (albeit rather ambivalently) toward becoming an independent person. Therefore, the recommendation given at the end of the diagnostic consultation phase was individual therapy for Linda and a series of sessions with the parents with the declared purpose of giving them support, but with the real intent of protecting their daughter's therapy.

The first few sessions with the parents were scheduled at the normal month interval. However, as therapy progressed, there emerged, at first in a rather disguised manner and, later on, in a more open manner, matrimonial problems that ruined the picture of closeness and solidarity that they had at first projected. They appeared bewildered and confused as they began, after having held back for years, to have ever more courage to accuse and reproach each other explicitly. There emerged, on the part of both of them, a sincere wish to get to the bottom of their problems. This led us to change the context of the therapy. The opportunity afforded the couple to concentrate entirely on their relationship permitted the daughter to free herself from her dependence on them and thus bring her therapy to a close with satisfactory results.

We have now mentioned a number of situations which, on principle as well as because of circumstances, impelled us to attempt a new therapeutic experience even though we lacked a clearly defined work project that would lead to theoretical and clinical/practical generalizations. Only later on did we begin to reflect upon the meaning of the choices we had made and on the results of the clinical work with couples. We arrived at the conclusion that, as a general rule, it was useful to adopt the individual-therapy setting for *all* couples, those who come from family therapy as well as those who explicitly request couples therapy. This decision involves considerably more time and energy, but the results are much more gratifying.

When we state that the couple presents problems and characteristics that are closer to those of the individual than to those of the family, we do not mean to generalize without making distinctions or to banalize or simplify a picture that is actually quite complex. The principal difficulty in dealing with couples is in managing the therapeutic relationship, and this is even more difficult in an individual-therapy context. It is as if each member of the couple felt as if he/she was in a context of individual therapy and thus had a privileged relationship with the therapist. This generates a complex, problematic situation with regard to the principle of neutrality, that is, the therapist is the therapist of both of the two members, and therefore, by definition, is allied with each of them. The pragmatic consequence of this is that the relationship with the therapist can become a strategical pawn between the members of the couple, with each attempting to exploit the therapist within the symmetrical pattern that the two of them have established.

What happens then is that the therapist is triangulated. Using overt or not so overt maneuvers, each partner seeks an alliance, hoping that his/her ideas will be backed up by the therapist. Thus the therapist often finds that he/she has to neutralize the demands for an alliance that would force him/her to side with one or the other of the members of the couple instead of analyzing the different points of view present in the system. The role requested of the therapist is that of a judge or a referee of a quarrel whose subject is of little importance. As J. Haley (1971) amply illustrated, the partners use any pretext, from discussing the latest theory of astrophysics to which detergent gets the wash whiter, to fight for the upper hand in their relationship. The question is a structural one of relationship, and not of content. It is natural that in a game whose stakes are so very high the members of the couple would very aggressively attempt to "seduce" the therapist.

Simon and Martha had requested therapy because, due to their frequent fights, they had postponed moving in together, even though the house that they had bought had been ready for more than a year. (We are purposely omitting any comment on the pragmatic meaning of the symptom.) During the session, they had very civilly discussed the different points of view that had sparked the furious arguments, which had rather painful consequences; delineated their problem; tried to understand the motives of the other; thoroughly considered every request of the therapist; and remained equidistant from the therapist. It was only at the end of the session, at the door of the therapy room, that they "let go." It was then that they asked the therapist trivial questions totally disconnected from the subjects discussed in the session—the intent was clearly that of winning the game that had just concluded. Their questions consisted of inconsequential matters (which, however, were important inside of their relationship) on which their opinions diverged markedly, instigating the ritual of their fights. We cite a few examples.

Simon: Doctor, how do you say it: shut the umbrella or close the umbrella? [Martha was in the habit of saying "shut the umbrella" and Simon was always telling her that this was a linguistic error.]

Martha: Doctor, we'll send you a postcard, because Saturday we are going away to the beach for . . . uh, how do you say it . . . a weekend. That's correct, isn't it? We're only going for 2 days. [Martha often pointed out to Simon that the term *weekend* should only be used to indicate a 2-day vacation, taken on Saturday and Sunday, whereas Simon used the word to mean a short vacation, which could be even 4 or 5 days long.]

Simon (pointing to Martha's purse): Excuse me, according to you, what is this thing?

Therapist: Martha, what does Simon mean? Why did he ask me that question?

Martha: Because he is always telling me that it is not a purse! He says that I fill it up so much that it looks more like a hiker's backpack than anything else. The other day we got into an awful fight about this purse.

Therapist: OK, I think that next time we ought to talk about precisely this matter.

Being the therapist allied with both members of the couple, as well as having an individual-therapy type relationship with each, means that the therapist must be ready to listen to both of them, even outside of the therapy setting. Whereas in family therapy, the therapist must not have any separate contact with the individual members of the system, in couples therapy, the therapist cannot avoid having this type of contact. The therapist is felt to be a privileged listener by both members, and it is not unusual for each frequently to test the real availability of the therapist with telephone calls or requests for separate, individual sessions. The solution to this problem lies in dosing out separate interventions and establishing what may well be a delicate, though not impossible, equilibrium. During the session, the therapist also has the opportunity to make fruitful use, in an indirect way, of the information gathered from the individual members of the couple, without compromising the private nature of the communication or professional secrecy.

Apart from this crucial point, which is the most problematic and typical aspect of couples therapy, we use the same intervention techniques for couples therapy as we do for individual therapy. The same rules and principles are valid for both. The technique of circular questions can again be used in the most fruitful manner, since with the couple one can immediately verify the retroaction of each partner with regard to the definition of the other member.

Held to be valid also in couples therapy are the rules of respect for the individuals' assumptions and the neutrality of the therapist with regard to the couple's common worldview. The couple, like any other system, shares a common worldview, which overlaps, or is at a metalevel with respect to the individual worldviews of each of the system's members. We would like to close the subject by citing one last case which illustrates the neutrality of the therapist toward the couple's worldview.

A childless couple, married for 12 years, came to us with a problem of sexual perversion on the husband's part, which the wife had discovered shortly after they were married. The man, the proprietor of a store, was 37 years old. He had developed the habit of putting on women's clothing and masturbating in front of a mirror. It was a ritual he repeated every day after closing up his shop. His wife discovered this habit when she found, by chance, her

husband's extensive wardrobe of women's clothing. However, the latter's sexual performance, while infrequent and
entered into with little emotional involvement, had not,
up until this time, been the object of his wife's complaints.
The 35-year-old wife, a very pretty ex-model, suffe-
redfrom such acute vaginismus that, in order to have
sexual relations, she had to take large doses of Valium.
Although they had these sexual problems (which, after all,
counterbalanced one another), the couple was very close in
all other respects and united by deep love for one another.
Not even the wife's unpleasant discovery had corroded
their relationship. Both of them had adapted to the situation, which responded to their joint need, that is, to avoid
unsatisfactory and problematic sexual relations. In this tacit
agreement, they had found an equilibrium, which had
remained stable up until the day the wife had confided her
husband's particular tastes to a few close woman friends.
This caused problems for the couple insofar as their perception of their relationship's normality was called into
question when the wife's friends insisted that she was
abnormal for having remained living with a man who was
so inadequate in his masculine role. In their opinion, she
needed to go for individual therapy. She accepted their
advice, and started therapy twice, both times abandoning
it after the first session. On both occasions she had been
told that it would be a good idea for her to separate from
her husband. That was definitely not her intention.

When the couple applied to us for therapy, their explicit
request to us was to help them overcome their sexual difficulties in order to conceive a child, which they had all of a sudden
begun to desire. Actually, their covert request was a recognition of their marital relationship as normal, since outside
prejudices had made them doubt this. It was immediately clear
that the conception of a child was a false problem. Neither of
the two seemed seriously motivated to have a child. On the
other hand, what more convincing proof of their normality
could they present to other people?

Thus, the couple requested of us a confirmation of their
marriage relationship and a recognition of their vision of the

world, which, though potentially assailable from a subjective point of view, was absolutely coherent with the epistemology and needs of both of them.

Our work with this couple was not aimed at changing them (after all, the husband's symptom had been a part of his personality since the age of 5 years old), but to analyze their decision to have a child and to reconstruct their shattered equilibrium and reassure the system.

Chapter 9

SYSTEMIC PSYCHOTHERAPY

FROM THE SYSTEM TO THE INDIVIDUAL

For the past decade, the systemic field has described a *system* as a complex, organized unit. This description emphasizes its totality. It is the antithesis of the idea of breaking the system down into its components. Thus, the operation of a system is seen more as a function of its type of organization than as a function of the properties of its components.

Breaking a system down into its components is useful for understanding how a nonliving system works. (Such a system may well be a complicated system, but it is not a complex one.) However, in biological and social systems, it is the cooperation of the components that gives the system, as a whole, new features (Bateson 1979).

It was by changing the focus of attention from the parts to the whole (in our case, from individuals to the family) that systemic thinkers came to hold these ideas, which are now shared by everyone in the field. This development took place in the 1960s and 1970s, during the years of great expansion in the field of family therapy.

However, thinking about a system only as a whole entailed

a risk whose consequence was similar to that connected with its antithesis, that is, reductionism. It was easy to lose sight of the distinctiveness of its component elements, thus to eliminate very important information. The nodes of a network of relationships cannot be disregarded (even though it is primarily their interconnection that makes them meaningful). This is even more important in the case in which these nodes are persons.

The next step in the thinking of systemic scholars was that of renewed interest in the variety and differentiation of the elements of the given system, in addition to its totality (Morin 1977). For us, as well as for other systemic therapists, this step, in effect, meant focusing on the individual in the system to which he/she belongs, stressing personal characteristics as well as those pertinent to the organization of the family. When we finally "perceived" the individuals within the family, the result was what we feel to be important technical and strategic changes in our way of doing therapy. (See section on the present, Chapter 2.) Another practical result of this rediscovery of the individual was that we began again to take into consideration, for various patients, the option of individual therapy.

It seemed to us that the principle of complementarity of different levels of observation of the same object of study would be especially valid for our clinical practice. Observing a given system as a whole, then focusing on its constituent parts, and, subsequently, once again considering the system as a whole, in a circular process, enriches our knowledge and renders more meaningful any given system's ongoing interactions and communicative behaviors.

We are convinced that it does not matter where one starts: by observing the whole or by observing the parts. Giving the proper emphasis to the elements of a system does not mean ignoring the importance of the system as a whole. The components of a system and the system as a global unit are not antithetical to each other but are, instead, two complementary viewpoints, which, ideally, should be integrated. We feel that the systemic model is of great advantage for the observation of a system and that it is the most suitable one for translating the results of a complex observation of a system into a recommendation for subsequent therapeutic treatment.

As distinct from some other models, which are not transferable to a context that is different from their original one (for example, the psychoanalytic model), our model offers the advantage of allowing us to work at all possible levels: the family, the individual, the couple. While systemic therapy in each of these three areas has its own specific technical characteristics, they are all based on the same principles and have a common methodology. This seems to us the genuinely unique and innovative feature of the systemic model.

We have come to these conclusions gradually, by discovering, one by one, the various viewpoints for the observation of any given system. Restricting the application of the systemic model to family therapy was really reductive, and this greatly limited our possibilities for doing therapy. When we became aware that, up until that time, we had underutilized the systemic model and underestimated its potentialities, we began taking into consideration courses of therapy other than family therapy. We began to sense and to test the possibilities of transferring the principles and rules of family therapy to another context, applying them to a very special system: the individual.

Viewing the individual as a system does not simply refer to the idea of the individual as a multicellular unit, having intracellular and intercellular chemical and physical processes, which are continuously carried out in an autonomous manner. The nervous system of human beings not only allows for a range of behaviors and relationships with the environment, but also makes it possible for the individual to enter into a relationship with himself/herself, that is, with his/her internal states (Maturana and Varela 1980). This peculiarity allows for the activation of mental processes. Therefore, every individual stands for (or can stand for) a complete network of relationships, including both the external and the internal, which determines his/her distinctive organization and defines his/her identity, social as well as biological.

The consideration of the individual as a system, making use of typically systemic categories (such as structure, organization, interactional domains) to guide us in the observation of the individual, did not necessitate our delineating a new model for therapy. It was sufficient to adapt the general principles already established for our family practice to the context of individual therapy. This proved to be an easy, spontaneous process. Various details pertaining to the therapy room, duration of therapy, and the frequency of the sessions had to be readjusted. However, no basic aspect of the clinical model, which we were using for family therapy, was altered.

Gradually, by the time that individual therapy done by family therapists had become fairly common practice (albeit without a clearly delineated basic model), we had become convinced that it was possible to apply our model to individual therapy. Doing individual therapy based on the systemic model was the natural result of our awareness that this model could be utilized in a broader manner by applying it to types of therapy other than family therapy. Therefore, this step did not seem like a break from our past clinical experience.

ADAPTING OUR MODEL

Applying the systemic model to individual therapy required only touching up a model that already existed and adapting it to a different context rather than creating or inventing a new model. We want to stress that it is not necessary to establish new principles and different rules from those which we already normally utilize in our family therapy practice. Our problem, instead, is that of formal recognition, by systemic therapists, of individual systemic therapy.

Probably, family therapists have always also done individual therapy. However, for many years they have been doing this second activity "behind closed doors." Naturally, this situation of people working in isolation has not favored the evolution of a unitary, clearly defined, formalized model. Too much time has gone by without ideas being circulated and without experiences being communicated and shared. The result is that we have only fragmentary material and therefore cannot describe a systemic model of individual therapy that could be universally recognized.

Although many isolated attempts have been reported in this field, valid as they may well be, they are probably not transferrable. Every therapist has put together techniques and personal strategies, which unfortunately have not been tested and compared.

In Italy, many family therapists are now utilizing individual therapy together with family therapy and are describing the methods and objectives of these strategies. In this sphere a debate is already going on, with various different positions and points of view represented. Some of these therapists (including our group) use these two techniques separately, although often simultaneously, with separate therapists for each different system. Others alternate family sessions (with the whole family or with a subsystem) with individual sessions (with a member of the system) without changing therapists (Selvini Palazzoli et al. 1989).

The subject which has not yet been adequately discussed is the utilization of individual systemic therapy as an alternative not only to family therapy but also to other types of individual therapy (psychoanalytic, cognitive, behavioristic, and so forth). Perhaps this is due to the fact that there is not yet an agreed-upon, standard model of individual systemic therapy.

Perhaps many systemic therapists feel embarrassed because they have only rather sketchy ideas on the matter, which are, perhaps, the fruits of eclecticism or improvisation. While we believe that at times, a good therapist can make up for a lack of specific techniques and a conceptual base with intuition and a ready heart, we feel it is generally fundamental to have a theoretical model as the basis for therapy. For us, this theoretical basis is the systemic model of family therapy. It seems obvious to us that, since the basic background for all systemic therapists is family therapy, one must extract from that context the principles, standards, and rules on which to base individual systemic therapy, adapting them to this different situation. This adaptation, however, does entail a change in the amount of time necessary for therapy as well as in the frequency of the therapeutic sessions.

Working with all of the members of a given family allows for gathering information in a relatively short amount of time, since one can immediately grasp the differences in punctuation, the retroactions, and the important aspects of communication within this family system. The structure and nature of these relationships come to light during the course of the two consultation sessions, making it possible to plan an appropriate intervention, which can be carried out in a limited number of sessions. (We rarely need more than ten sessions for family therapy.) However, when it is impossible to check the different points of view and grasp the relational aspects of communication by circular questioning in the therapy session, relatively more time is necessary to obtain the same results. On the basis of our experience, we would estimate that fifteen to twenty sessions of individual therapy correspond to one session of family therapy in terms of therapeutic effect. The average duration of individual therapy (eighty to ninety sessions) is about a year and a half, which is more or less equal to the duration of family therapy, taking into account the frequency of the sessions.

The average interval of a month between family therapy sessions is necessary to allow the system to utilize the therapeutic interventions to effect changes in structure (Selvini Palazoli 1980). Natural evolution is a factor in the history of human systems; therefore, the factor of time must be duly considered: change that is too rapid can be destructive. It is necessary to allow the system to evolve, giving it time to get its bearings with respect to the perturbations and to regain a more stable equilibrium after a temporary destabilization. A suspension of therapy for 2 or 3 months will not compromise the relationship between therapist and family; and, at times, it is even fruitful in the therapeutic process and could be intentionally prescribed as a strategic move. This is not the case in individual therapy, in which the ideal interval between sessions seems to be a week's time. This time interval is not so long that the patient feels abandoned, nor is it too short to permit the patient to reelaborate the material that has come to light in the session and to utilize the restructuring interventions of the therapist.

Another feature that distinguishes individual therapy from family therapy in our practice is the therapy room. The room does not have the one-way mirror, video camera, and intercom. It is a normal professional office, and the therapeutic situation is face-to-face. This environment eliminates the possibility of contemporaneous supervision.

We are aware that many therapists work with individuals in a family-therapy setup, or at least with videotaping, though without contemporaneous supervision. We believe that these different procedures are based on principles that are different from those that we will present in the next section. Our staff has a well-defined conception of individual systemic therapy with regard to theory, methodology, and techniques, which need to be explained in detail.

Often the question about how the systemic therapist does individual therapy is dealt with in a perfunctory manner by asserting that doing systemic therapy means dealing with the relationships of the patient. This statement is not specific enough, since it is applicable to any type of psychotherapeutic treatment. It is inevitable that when a process of change is set into motion in the individual, the relational networks of which the patient is part are modified as well. If this definition is accepted as a valid one, it must be completed by the explanation of how one deals with these relationships. What kind of strategies and therapeutic tools does a systemic therapist utilize? How can these be utilized in individual therapy?

COMMON PREMISES WITH FAMILY THERAPY

Before going further into detail in describing our intervention techniques and the problems associated with them, we would like to talk about the differentiation of our conception of individual therapy from its origins, family therapy. It seems to us that one could describe this process in terms of belonging and individualization: a progressive independence from its own roots that neither underrates these roots nor is unfaithful to them. For this reason, we would like to emphasize that for us, individual systemic therapy is not simply family therapy done also with or exclusively through a single member of the system. In our practice, this is therapy of the individual for the individual.

For various other workers in the field, individual systemic therapy resembles family therapy or, at least, is part of a broader strategy of the same type. The idea of being able to work on the system through one of its members is supported by the premise that each component recapitulates in itself the rules of the system to which he/she belongs, displays the same organizing traits, and tends to reestablish with the therapist the types of significant relationships established with the other members within his/her family system (Loriedo et al. 1989). We do not share this point of view. We have learned from synergetics that the observation of a system on a macroscopic level reveals properties that have to do only with the system as a whole and which cannot be found in its components. The type of organization of a system and its mechanisms of functioning cannot be totally grasped unless the global configuration is studied. It is true that by interacting with a single element of a system and by inquiring into the relationships that this member has with the others, one can make various hypotheses. However, we feel that one cannot verify these hypotheses without working with the whole family. We continue to require the presence of all of the members of the family when doing family therapy.

When we are doing individual therapy, we do not allow communication with members of the family other than the patient. Any type of interference is immediately nipped in the bud. In this respect, we are not different from therapists who adhere to other models of individual therapy.

Very often there are telephone calls or requests for a meeting made by parents who have a child in therapy. However, it is not rare for a spouse to interfere with regard to the therapy of his/her partner, or even for a son or daughter with regard to therapy of a parent. Any attempt of this type is is reported to the patient and discussed in the session. The therapist's relationship with the patient remains exclusive; it is only with him/her that the therapist defines a sphere of work and a relational space with clearly established limits. We feel that this is a fundamental rule to observe in order to assure a good therapeutic outcome. It is for this reason that we feel that is necessary, in cases of parallel interventions, to keep the context of individual therapy separate from that of family therapy. We found that every time that, for some reason or another, we violated this rule of separation of contexts, the therapeutic work was damaged, at times irreparably.

An error on the part of the therapist has a different type of effect in the two different contexts. In family therapy, errors are more easily rectified; in individual therapy, they are almost always irremediable. In family therapy, one can reread an intervention that has turned out to be inadequate, or one can resolve an impasse, by using the supervisor in a strategic manner. For example, one can, at times, attribute to the supervisor a different point of view from that held by the acting therapist, as though there were a sort of split in the therapeutic staff's viewpoint with regard to the given subject. However, in individual therapy, the therapist is totally responsible for all decisions and therapeutic options and thus must be in absolute control over what he/she does and says. Contemporaneous supervision facilitates the timely recognition of the therapist's errors and wrong moves. This is not the case with individual-therapy supervision, which takes place after the fact. In the family-therapy context, the presence of all of the components of the given system makes it possible to immediately check the retroactions of the therapeutic interventions. In individual therapy, however, it is necessary to reconstruct, after the fact, how the patient has manipulated the therapeutic intervention for effecting any restructuring and how he/she has utilized it in relationships with significant others.

Another feature of contemporaneous supervision is, or used to be when it was utilized as a function of control, that it limits the therapist's involvement with the family. Aside from the presence of the supervisor, the family therapist has at his/her disposal a number of techniques, of which neutrality is one, which permit him/her to resolve problems of transference. In individual therapy, the therapist is, by definition, allied with the patient. Involvement, within certain limits, is inevitable. Therefore, it is necessary to take into account transference and countertransference, even though, working at a level that is not as deep as that worked on by psychoanalysis and psycho-analytically oriented therapy, the management of these tendencies is simpler.

Thus, it would seem to be easier to do family therapy than to do individual therapy! Working as part of a group does give one a feeling of security, and if the group is a close one, it makes for a less anxiety-producing environment.

THEORETICAL AND CLINICAL FEATURES
OF THE MODEL

Our model of individual therapy has a body of theoretical principles and pragmatic aspects in common with family therapy. One of the fundamental assumptions shared by these two contexts is that one works in the here and now, without reexperiencing the various stages of emotional and cognitive development which are the foundation for adult life and for the life stage in which we are called upon to step in.

We do not work on *why* but rather on *how*. We draw on explicative schemes that do not have linear cause-and-effect chains. There are events and behaviors; and these take on significance only in the reciprocal interaction between two or more individuals. Therefore, we are interested in understanding and analyzing how the patient's family and social relationships are structured at the time when he/she requests therapy and what kind of distress is connected with, though not caused by, these relationships. The generic expression *work on relationships* could apply to our work in this sense: we read the distress and suffering in terms of current relationships, without referring to events that might have touched off the distress or to traumas in the past.

However, it often happens that the patients themselves bring up these events. They recount episodes that they feel are significant or report memories, establishing precise connections between various experiences (even those from long ago) and their symptoms. People are almost always interested in reconstructing their past, and when they are in therapy, they feel stimulated to go through the various stages again, presenting to the therapist a series of rationalizations having to do with their disturbance and their symptoms that are so crystalized as to be difficult to dismantle. On the other hand, it can also happen that, when an individual requests therapy, he/she does not have a clear perception of his/her own problems. This patient may simply experience a state of distress and ask the therapist for help in identifying the problems. Often, the people who live in contact with the patient are unaware of the latter's distress and may not even know about the ongoing therapy.

Our main objective is not to act directly upon the symptom through strategic and paradoxical interventions, but rather to take apart and reconstruct the premises, that is, the basic assumptions, of the patient by proposing alternate hypotheses. We feel that an intervention that is limited to dealing with the symptom is, after all, a technical maneuver, which is inherently limited and risks not resolving the problem in a definitive manner. We prefer to aim at more than a temporary remission of the symptom(s). Our goal is a stable restructuring of the individual-system, which might take the form of a firmly changed perception of the problem.

We have found it advantageous to offer various different readings of a given situation or communicative interchange. Alternative punctuations can be proposed by questions like "Haven't you ever thought that your husband intended to express his appreciation of you by that particular behavior?" or "Could it possibly be that on that occasion your mother used her suffering to communicate something to your father?"

The patient surely has formulated his/her own hypotheses about various subjects, and some of these may be very solidly structured. The therapist offers others, which may turn out to contribute to restructuring by introducing new meanings for interactions and observed behaviors. The main objective of the therapeutic intervention is to give the patient the opportunity to experience a novel way of understanding certain sequences of past events and observed behaviors, rather than to heighten the patient's consciousness with regard to his/her relationships and communicative interchanges. We do not believe that the therapist necessarily has to surprise the patient with a sensational intervention. However, an intervention is effective in restructuring insofar as it broadens the patient's point of view. Nonetheless, an intervention must be in harmony with the individual's epistemology in the sense that it is constructed by taking into account the patient's basic assumptions, and his/her capacity for reelaboration. Even in individual therapy we tend to co-construct our therapeutic interventions with the patient. Explanations and rationalizations are of no use. One must create a learning context. We consider the therapeutic experience as a learning II experience (in the Batesonian sense of the term) (Bateson 1972), which is transferable to other contexts and which produces change. In this way, the individual-system should be able to overcome the rigidity that trapped him/her in a one-way view of reality—that is, in linear schemes of thought that connected events and behaviors to precise causes—and thus he/she should become more flexible.

This learning experience does not come about at a pragmatic level, through behavioral indications by the therapist. In family therapy, the therapist tends to be directive and also makes use of prescriptions. In individual therapy, the therapist accompanies the patient on the road toward autonomy and change, without any imposition. He/she restricts himself/herself to proposing new descriptions of the same sequences of events that "perturb" the patient. These descriptions can then be utilized by the individual in his/her development.

Remaining neutral with regard to the various possible punctuations is often very difficult because patients tend to ask direct questions. To avoid giving answers as direct as the questions often requires a great deal of tact. Patients consider their therapists experts and consultants. Therefore, they expect to receive direction and useful advice as well as an antidote for their distress, and they explicitly ask for these things.

The therapist does not meet these expectations, and thus does not take the place of the patient in making pragmatic decisions. However, the therapist must discharge two specific functions. The first is to unconditionally accept the request of the patient, whatever it is and however incongruent it may be with the therapist's mental and ethical categories. The therapist must not question the morality of the individual needs that are expressed by the patient. He/she can only turn them into objects of analysis and verification, in order to steer the patient, if possible, toward other points of view. We feel that this feature of the therapist's work is similar to the technique of positive connotation that is used in family therapy. It is a technique for rereading any behavior, even symptoms, as positive and as effective for some purpose as well as a way of communicating something. The request for therapy and the motivations behind the request are also communications, which should be accepted without reservations.

> An extreme case, which illustrates this topic, is that of a bank official who requested therapy from one of the authors of this book in order to acquire the "psychological strength" to carry off a bank robbery, which he had long since planned, at the bank where he worked. The therapist, playing along with him, took a year and a half to analyze together with the patient in meticulous detail all of the steps necessary to execute this plan and, at the same time, the underlying motivations and needs expressed by the project and the request for therapy. Therapy was concluded when the patient, through an independent, though guided, process, had acquired the capacity to see, this time "through different lenses," his real needs, his expectations, and his attitude toward his profession. By the time therapy ended, the patient had retired to the countryside where he owned some land to manage his property.

The second function of the therapist is to carefully comment on the material that the patient brings to the therapy session, as well as on his/her own observations, perceptions, and emotions. The therapist must not question the patient's world outlook on the basis of his/her own personal categories of judgment; however, he/she is obliged to express an opinion about the effectiveness and adequacy of the means and ways that the patient has planned to use or has already used to translate his/her attitudes, hopes, and needs into concrete actions. One could say that the therapist must formulate a technical appraisal that the patient can use in changing his/her world outlook.

The therapist's comments also include metacommunications about the patient's relationships, including the therapeutic relationship. The careful observation of the communicative aspects of every event and behavior and the therapist's restructuring response to the patient allow the individual-system and his/her relationship network to evolve over the course of time.

Patients repeatedly make attempts to force the therapist to define himself/herself with respect to a subject or problem. In similar situations, splitting can be an effective technique in handling the situation. If a patient who is at an impasse about a decision asks for clarification, the therapist can reply that the patient's proposed solution seems suitable, but, at the same time, implies taking a number of risks. This type of attitude induces the patient to take responsibility for his/her own decisions and to engage his/her personal resources.

Another stratagem that a therapist can use to avoid giving a direct answer or expressing a personal opinion is to refer to the cases he/she has seen, rather than to the categories that pertain to his/her worldview or personal experiences or feelings. Even more important, the therapist must remain neutral, avoiding value judgments in his/her comments and metacommunications. Of course, the word *neutrality* has a different meaning in individual therapy. It is not the resultant sum (zero) of the interventions in which the therapist has allied himself/herself with the various members of the system as in family therapy. However, we can speak of neutrality as a rule also in individual therapy if we refer to the therapist's abstention from giving practical advice and opinions on decisions and from making value judgments.

The technique of circularity also had to be adapted to the context of individual therapy. The principle is still valid. However, the standard three-individual question cannot be made, nor is it possible to have an immediate verification of the retroactions of the other members involved in relationships with the patient. The hypothetical questions that we consider circular (even if there is only one member of the system in conversation with the therapist) are always a special source of information, able to highlight the meaningful differences. Questions such as "What do you think that your wife thought when . . . ?" or "What do you think your wife would think and do if . . . ?" have the drawback of the answer's not being immediately verifiable, but they leave room for the expression of the patient's beliefs and suppositions. The answers that take the form of suppositions about the opinions and communicative objectives of other persons are true definitions of relationships in the sense that they give information about the type and quality of the relationships that the patient has established with these persons. A certain amount of time is necessary to gather this information: the process of using circular questions for the reconstruction of a global picture is like putting together a puzzle, piece by piece. Nevertheless, the repetition of the circular questions during the course of therapy and the careful comparison of the answers does allow verification of the definitions of relationships given by the patient at different times and of the retroactions of other members of the patient's family, even though it requires more time than it does in family therapy.

THE CLINICAL PROCESS

We feel that it would be worthwhile now to call upon some of our already numerous patients to speak. (We have recorded the therapy sessions from which the following extracts come with a normal audiocassette recorder.) Our patients are the main protagonists of our therapeutic experience, which has at times been marked by enthusiasm and confidence, and at other times, instead, by doubt and uncertainty; but it has always been very stimulating.

We feel that the facts should be given more weight than theoretical explanations and abstract examples. Therefore, we will present a few clinical cases, those which we feel were most significant in training us to become systemic individual therapists, or, perhaps, simply, those which were most significant to us emotionally. We are aware that we have received more from these patients than we have given them. It was with them that we constructed a new view of reality, had fond relationships, and shared fears, anxieties, hopes, and satisfactions. For these reasons we are quite sure that these patients were the principal creators of our therapeutic successes.

We will not write about our failures, because we believe that they are mainly due to our errors of evaluation and of application and to our personal limitations, rather than to defects of the basic therapeutic model.

SEARCHING FOR A LOST FATHER

Seventeen-year-old Denise was the eldest child of her family in which there was also a 13-year-old brother. She was a very vivacious teenager, with an active social life, and was forever in search of new experiences. Denise's "curiosity," which her very conservative and traditional-istic parents had always viewed with disfavor, often led her into situations in which she violated the norms of her parents. Denise was considered to be at risk for social maladjustment and had been labeled as delinquent by her family, especially by her mother, and by the various social service professionals whose help Denise's mother had sought at different times. Denise had also been labeled a drug addict because she smoked marijuana on occasion. Denise persistently rejected the label of social deviant, feeling that she had no need of being "rehabilitated." She came to our Center with her parents, who had requested our help in managing their daughter. She had abandoned her studies three months prior to the time of her first visit. However, she was in no hurry to find a job. She had a boyfriend with whom she went out in the evening. She came home from these dates in the small hours of the morning, causing her parents no end of worry. They cited a number of incidents in which she had been involved, among which were a car accident, an arrest when she was drunk, and a riot during a concert.

Denise described her relationship with her mother as very conflictual—full of arguments, scenes, insults—and her relationship with her father as practically nonexistent except for those occasions on which, provoked by his wife (who exasperated him with her complaints about Denise), he would hit his daughter. Her image of her mother was that of a person who was anxious by nature and always worried about the safety of her daughter. Denise's mother attributed her supposed cardiological problems to these worries.

At the end of the consultation with the whole family, we decided to take on the parents and to propose indi-vidual therapy to Denise, adhering to Denise's punctuation and thus removing the label of problem child. The therapists said that they did not feel that Denise needed to be "rehabilitated," but rather that she needed to be helped to understand and to resolve the problems in her relationship with her parents (which did not necessarily depend only upon her). This motivation for therapy made it possible to engage Denise without any difficulty after two consultation sessions, the second of which was divided into two parts: one with the whole family and one with Denise alone. What follows is the conversation of the engagement phase.

Therapist: The impression that my colleagues and I have is that you are suffering, that you are in difficulty, and that you are in need of help. Let me explain what I mean. We do not feel that you are in need of being "rehabilitated." You are simply a teenager who has the needs and expectations characteristic of adolescents. Your attitude is a bit reactive and a bit rebellious, but that is normal for a person of your age, which is an age in which the rules imposed by adults sometimes seem unacceptable. However, we feel that you are a very intelligent person, that you are full of resources, and that you know what you want without needing others to tell you. Nonetheless, it seems to us that right now you are having difficulties managing your relationship with your parents and that, in this area, you are in need of help. We are not particularly interested in knowing who is to blame for this situation. Usually, in this kind of situation, everybody shares some of the responsibility. We would like to try to understand why it is so hard to manage to get along and to find some way to resolve the problem of conflict in your relationship with your parents. It is in this sense that talking with a therapist might help you. At the same time, we would continue to see your parents to work with them, because they, too, need help. What do you think of this?

Denise: Well, to tell you the truth, I didn't want to come to the Center because I'm not like they say I am, and all that's required for things to be clarified in our family is a bit of effort. But now I think that maybe it's worthwhile . . . but I don't think that my way of seeing things is wrong. I don't want to be changed.

Therapist: Do you think that that's what we want to do? To change you?

Denise: Uh, I don't know. . . .

Therapist: We think that you need help in getting a handle on your relationship with your parents. That's what our aim is. What makes it especially important is the fact that you are suffering. You are very involved in this relationship; it's clear that you have very close emotional ties to your family. We have understood this from the things that you have told us. You have spoken several times about being concerned about your mother, your father, and your brother—if they were not important to you, you wouldn't be concerned about them, but it is clear that you *are* upset.

Denise: Yes, that's right. I would like to feel comfortable with my family, but I don't want to give up my ideas. . . . I don't know what to do.

Therapist: You see, Denise, this is exactly what you could try to understand with the help of another person.

Denise: OK, so how do I go about doing this?

One must not consider this alliance with the patient as a mere strategic maneuver made simply to engage the identified patient. This alliance was consistent with the hypothesis that had gradually come into focus during the two consultation sessions. The therapists had perceived that, even though Denise had a very reactive attitude toward her parents, she was eager to have a good relationship with them. Denise seemed to have a very clear view of reality. She was even objective enough to recognize that certain of her parents' expectations were justifiable. She gave us a very definite impression of "being present" in the relationship with them in spite of the difficulties of the situation. She also went along with them without protesting every time they decided on some kind of intervention on her behalf, since, as she herself wanted to emphasize, she wanted to prove to them that she wasn't a "wrong 'un." This hypothesis was confirmed during the course of individual therapy, an extract from the third session of which follows.

Denise: We are all suffering in this situation, . . . however, *I* can get away from it. I go out with my friends and do things I enjoy doing. My parents have it worse, because they can't get away from it.

Therapist: What you are saying is that you are more worried about them than you are about yourself, right?

Denise: Right . . . and I feel sorry for them. I want them to understand that I am an "OK person," but they insist that they want me to do whatever they decide upon. They want to change me, but it's just not possible. . . . I ought to try to meet them halfway, maybe answer back less and keep my mouth shut more often.

Therapist: Do you think that this would make your parents more understanding of you?

Denise: No, not more understanding, but at least less apprehensive. My mother is awfully insistent; she is always on my back. The more I run away from the situation, the more they run after me. . . .

Therapist: How do you think the situation could be unblocked?

Denise (speaking hesitantly): I don't know. Maybe I could avoid running away from it so often. If our relationships at home were different . . . I don't know . . . well, if my mother were more friendly and my father less detached from the problems—because he always wants to stew in his own juices . . . he never wants to discuss things, to clarify the situation, my mother yells at me. She gets mad easily. Her character is like mine. Sometimes she feels ill, and she keels over. She says that these are heart attacks. . . .

Therapist: Are you frightened when this happens?

Denise: I used to be, but not any more. But it still upsets me.

Therapist: Do you feel that you are responsible when this happens?

Denise: Of course I do.

Therapist: How come you feel responsible? You say that you don't do weird things and that you aren't bad.

Denise: Well, because when we start to discuss things, we raise our voices, and we get upset, and then she starts feeling ill. I don't feel that I'm in the wrong, but I feel sorry about it, even if I'm just not able to keep my mouth shut. I prefer to discuss things, to argue. . . . Usually I raise my voice. We end up talking about the same things that she can't stand. She always rakes up the past. When she saw that I had changed, she began to see in me things that only she sees, and she began to get on my back.

Therapist: Years ago, when you were younger, did your mother keep after you like this?

Denise: No. Well, my mother was always very attached to me. I was born after twelve years. . . . For her, I was the most important thing in her life . . . yeah, even for my father, too. (A long pause.) Oh, and then there was the affair of my cousin who went into a therapeutic community because she was addicted to drugs. My mother then began to worry, even though I was still a small child, thinking that the same thing was going to happen to me. Sometimes she is ill, the situation is heavy, and I know that it's all my fault. . . .

Therapist: Why do you think it's all due to you? Things are never like that. The responsibility never belongs to just one person.

Denise: Well, it seems that whenever I'm involved, the whole family is involved. For instance, when I get into an argument with my mother, my brother gets involved, and then my mother gets angry at my father because she wants him to yell at me. . . .

Therapist: So, what does he do? Doe he yell at you or stick up for you?

Denise (lowering her voice): He doesn't do anything. . . . He thinks my mother is right . . . but anyway, even he feels bad about it. . . . Everybody suffers because everybody's involved.

Therapist: That's understandable. When people live together, everybody ends up taking part in things, everybody shares in things, and everybody is involved. But this doesn't depend only on you. Certainly your mother has her good reasons, but then, so do you. . . .

Our hypothesis was that Denise, rather than rebelling and defying her parents (as a prelude to detaching herself from them, which was possible, since she was but a few months away from being legally an adult), was, in effect, asking for her parents' recognition of her as a person; above all, she wanted to be accepted by them in spite of her turbulent adolescent behavior. We began to get the idea that Denise particularly wanted this recognition from her father.

Denise seemed quite ambivalent about her father. On the one hand, she accused him of hitting her and of not understanding her. On the other, she seemed to absolve him of responsiblity for the decisions taken with regard to her, placing it, instead, all on her mother. Even though, in this family, the father seemed to have a marginal role as far as his wife was concerned, Denise constantly drew attention to him. The disclosure of this information allowed the therapist to formulate a correct hypothesis and to stimulate Denise to reframe the situation, which turned out to be decisive in this case.

Denise: If I return late in the evening, my mother is always afraid that something (who knows what?) is going to happen to me — that I'm going to take drugs, that I'm going to land in the hospital, as if these things could only happen after midnight. . . .

Therapist: Do you think that your father also has these fears?

Denise: My father's never made it clear what, if anything, he fears. For better or for worse, I've always argued only with Mom. . . .

Therapist: But, Denise, do you have the impression that your father, even if he leaves it to your mother to take action, agrees with your mother with regard to what to do about you?

Denise: No. Even though Dad usually doesn't speak up, I often get the impression that he doesn't think the way Mom does. Mom is fussier, stubborner, and nastier with me than he is. Maybe he'd let some things pass. . . .

Therapist: So, why do you think he allows these things to go on if he doesn't think they should?

Denise (hesitantly): Maybe he's afraid to confront me.

Therapist: In what way might he be afraid to confront you? What exactly do you mean?

Denise (lowering her voice): Maybe he's afraid to lose me completely . . . to completely lose me.

Therapist: And why do you think he might be afraid of this?

Denise (on the verge of tears): I don't know. I can't understand my father's behavior. I don't think that it is simply because that's his nature, because he acts differently with Paul. I guess it depends on me. . . . I wish I could have a different kind of relationship with my father, and could discuss things with him, clarify things by talking about them. Maybe he isn't able to do that. . . .

Therapist: You think that he might find that difficult?

Denise: Yes, maybe he doesn't feel capable of discussing things with me. I don't know if it's a question of schooling or if it's something else.

Therapist: When you were as old as Paul is now, what was your father like?

Denise: When I was my brother's age, I didn't ever have problems at home.

Therapist: But what was your relationship with your father like at that time? From what you've said it seems like your father and Paul have something in common.

Denise: I'd have to say that when I was a small child, up to about the age Paul is now, my father absolutely adored me. There were never any arguments. There was never anything serious about which to argue.

Therapist: But what were *your* feelings about your father?

Denise (in a tone of voice that reveals the depth of the emotions that she is feeling): Well, I felt that we were closer. . . . (She begins to sob quietly.)

Therapist: Did you do things together?

Denise (attempting to regain control of herself, speaking with a steadier voice): Yes.

Therapist: Why do these memories make you feel so miserable?

Denise (giving way to crying): I don't know. . . .

Therapist: When you think about your relationship with your father, do you always feel like this?

Denise: Yes.

Therapist: Does it ever happen to you, when you think about your relationship with your mother, that you feel miserable and cry?

Denise: No. Never.

Therapist: How come?

Denise: Maybe because I never feel that I am missing my mother. Maybe it's that.

Therapist: What do you mean? Do you think that you've lost your father?

Denise (continuing to cry): No, but it is very difficult to get him back. But . . . I don't know . . . I've never before cried for my father.

Therapist: So, this is the first time, right?

Denise: Yes. It seems strange to me. . . .

Therapist: I see that this is a delicate subject, and it makes you feel miserable, even if you are not always aware of that.

Denise (her voice trembling): Yes, in fact, I really feel this lack quite a lot . . . and also the fact that he never speaks to me. When I bring him his coffee and he yells at me, I really feel unhappy then.

Therapist (starting to reframe the situation): Maybe he also feels unhappy. . . .

Denise (immediately perks up): Uh . . . yes, of course. . . .

Therapist: When he says, "I've already given up on Denise as a lost cause," why do you think he says that? What does he mean?

Denise: Maybe he suffers in silence, at least compared to my mother.

Therapist: Couldn't it be that when he says that, he's expressing a fear rather than an intention? The fear of losing you or of having lost you? Don't you think that that might be what he means?

Denise listens in silence.

Therapist: Don't you think it could be that your father, when he says this, is expressing his fear of having lost you and of not knowing how to get you back?

Denise: Maybe it's that.

Therapist: Maybe you and your father both have the same problem. You might both be convinced that the other has been lost, and you both feel the lack of the other. Maybe he isn't able to express it—although you, by crying, have expressed it—but you're not able to communicate it to each other.

Denise: Yes. Maybe that's the way it is.

Therapist: With your mother you have a more conflictual relationship. You argue, you fight, but certainly you manage to communicate your emotions to each other, and to confirm to each other that there are strong ties that bind you together. However, with your father, it seems that there is some difficulty in communicating this on an emotional level.

Denise: That's so.

Therapist: Maybe this is a problem that makes your father very anxious. Maybe he prefers to say, "I'm done with you, and I don't want to know anything more" rather than feel so miserable, the way you feel.

Denise (relieved): Yes, that's true. Often when I fought with my mother—before we started coming here to the Center—and he intervened by hitting me, I would hear him go into his room afterwards and cry. And yet it seems impossible that a person as big as he is could cry like that, and for such a little thing. . . . I felt worse hearing my father cry in bed like that than I did seeing my mother fall to the ground when she had palpitations.

Therapist: Certainly you and your mother communicate in a clearer way, even though there is disagreement between the two of you. You feel that you have a hold on your mother emotionally, while, instead, you feel that you've lost your father. Actually, that perception doesn't correspond to reality because, as you said before, maybe your father also has the same problem as you have, and he doesn't know how to get you back.

Denise: Yes, probably it's like that. However, already for the past few days, I've been seeing him in a different light. Maybe hope is not dead. . . . I guess there's always hope for everybody.

The therapist's reframing of the behavior of Denise's father made it possible for Denise to become aware of her needs and desires, as well as the means for attaining them. It also oriented Denise toward more suitable behavior. At the end of therapy (which lasted for a year and a half), Denise's relationship with her father had markedly improved. Denise had found a regular job, and had made a great change in her habits and in the hours she kept, coming closer to conforming to the expectations of her parents, even though she still insisted on having a certain degree of decisional autonomy.

A MYTH TO DEMOLISH

Julia was 38 years old when she applied for individual therapy. She had described the past 2 years as being like an interminable trek through the Russian mountains: "You climb up and then you fall, and then you climb again. . . . In the end, you don't know which is worse, the panic that accompanies the descent or the anxiety that after scaling the mountain you will still encounter a chasm."

She was referring to the period of time in which her daughter Deborah had been gravely ill with anorexia nervosa. This situation had made it necessary for Julia to give up her job, to which she had devoted much time and energy. It was, in fact, the first job she had had since she had graduated from college. She explained that she had been a homemaker until then as a result of having married at a tender age and not long afterwards given birth to her daughter.

During the hospitalization of her daughter a few months after the onset of the symptoms, Julia had been made to feel very guilty about her daughter's illness. The doctors in charge of her daughter told her that, as Deborah's mother, she was the sole cause of her daughter's eating disorder.

Julia's husband had implicitly reinforced that idea, since he had confronted that difficult time by asking for help from his mother-in-law instead of from his wife. Julia was left out of all of the decisions regarding her daughter, from the most important, such as whether or not to have Deborah treated in the hospital, to the most trivial, for example, planning the shifts of the various family members to stay with Deborah at the hospital.

The reason was that the family had always viewed Julia as a fragile and immature person, who was incapable of facing difficult situations that required courage.

Julia's family of origin had looked upon her as a fragile daughter to love and protect. When she got married, her husband regarded her as a wife to take care of and to shield from responsibilities. Actually, this belief had all of the characteristics of a family myth, the most important of which being that it was clearly not in line with the evidence. But nobody, not even Julia, seemed to realize this.

From Julia's descriptions, however, a very different image of the family emerged. Her husband, who was 10 years older than she, was a a music teacher who was depressed at the idea of forever giving individual music lessons and who constantly thought about teaching in the Conservatory and playing in an orchestra. In the past, he had competed several times for a place in the orchestra, but had never won one. Julia and the other famliy members attributed this fact to bad luck or not knowing the right people, rather than to lack of talent. Julia described her husband as an artist and a cultured person, although from her accounts of family life, he appeared to be a mediocre, if not dull, person.

Julia accepted, without protest, her husband's telling her which books to read, which exhibits to go to see, and so forth, because she felt incompetent to make these judgments, even though she had gone to a classic studies high school and done well there and also had a college degree in philosophy and arts.

Thus, the myth of Julia's inadequacies grew and was reinforced by the need to cover up the real inadequacies of her husband. We have selected the following extract from a therapy session in which Julia began to bring to light the family myth.

Julia: My parents were always very happy about my relationship with Stanley, even though when I met him I was still in my teens and he was already a mature person. They felt that he was exactly the right man for me, and, in fact, they were right. My husband has always given me a sense of security. You know, I'm rather unstable by nature.

Therapist: What do you mean?

Julia: I mean he's a very determined person. He knows what he wants and how to get it. He knows how to face up to difficult situations. I need somebody to give me advice and to guide me, because I quickly lose my nerve, and I see problems where they don't really exist. It's my nature. Instead of facing up to circumstances, I find that I'm overwhelmed by situations. I was like this even as a child.

Therapist: Do you mean that there's always been somebody to guide you?

Julia: Whether it's a good thing or not, yes, there's always been somebody.

Therapist: You've never taken the initiative on any matter?

Julia: Rarely, and only for unimportant things. But it doesn't bother me; it's actually helpful! Before I got married, I had my father to guide me. I had a lot of faith in him, maybe because we had the same opinions on most things. Afterwards, I had my husband. It was like he stood in for my father, because, actually, he has a rather particular kind of relationship with me. . . . When I joke with him, I say that he enjoys playing teacher with me! He is rather fatherly toward me . . . maybe it's also because of the age difference. . . . But this is an advantage, because my husband is a cultured person. For example, he advises me on which articles to read in the newspaper and which I can ignore because they're not worthwhile. Or else which films and which exhibits to go to see. . . .

Therapist: Doesn't it irritate you that your husband programs for you your interests and your reading, or directs your curiosity with regard to culture? After all, you have a college degree in the humanities and certainly you have the cultural background to be able to understand what's worthwhile reading!

Julia: Yes, but after graduating from college, I spent most of the time as a housewife. You know, after a while, you forget what you've studied, you get sort of rusty. . . . Besides, as I said before, there's nothing wrong with this, because I admire my husband. He's a musician, an artist.

Therapist: Exactly what kind of work does your husband do, in particular?

Julia: He teaches music to children in school, and he also gives private lessons. He's had rather bad luck. His dream was to play in an orchestra, but when there were competitions for openings, he never won. . . . He doesn't enjoy teaching school children. It would be different teaching at the Conservatory, but his is a normal school, not a music school. For him this is awfully frustrating!

Therapist: So, your husband never managed to win a place . . .

Julia (interrupting the therapist): But not for lack of ability! For these things you have to know people in high places and to be recommended by them. He's tried many times, but with no luck. I really feel sorry for him, because he could have had a splendid career!

Therapist: From what you've told me, it seems as if your husband is sort of a pillar in your life. And you, how do you guide your husband? How do you help him?

Julia: I? (half embarrassed, half amused): I couldn't say. . . . (A long silence follows.)

Therapist: Come on, try. In a couple, there is always, way down deep, some sort of tacit agreement, something of this sort: you give me a hand in this, I'll help you in that.

Julia: Well . . . maybe I'm the more practical person . . . you know, in household management, while from this point of view, he's not so great. Maybe in this sense I help him.

Therapist: Is that all?

Julia: Yes, I guess that's all.

Therapist: Julia, if I were to ask your daugher to tell me the areas in which you and your husband help each other, what do you think she'd say?

Julia: What I just told you, that is, that my husband gives me a feeling of security and moral support, while I'm the more practical one. But I don't know if you could really call this helping him—I said this more or less to give an answer, because your question caught me by surprise. Actually, I don't know if he'd consider that giving him a hand.

Julia had gradually come to the idea of going for therapy in the atmosphere of great insecurity that followed her euphoria over the recovery of her daughter. She had also gotten the idea that the hospital psychologist who met with her had had this in mind for her.

Julia's daughter had rapidly regained her health once she was discharged from the hospital. However, with regard to the relationship between mother and daughter, the situation was not so encouraging. Julia felt as though she were constantly the target of attacks by her daughter, even though she had gradually come to realize that this could also be the means that her daughter had adopted for approaching her. Sometimes it appeared as if Deborah were brushing up the tyrannical style of communication that had characterized her relationship with her mother in her anorexic phase.

Julia hoped that therapy would provide her with some kind of help in managing her relationship with her daughter during a period she felt to be precarious for both of them. In particular, she was in doubt as to what would be the most appropriate way to behave at times of crisis. She was very determined not to surrender to her daughter's petty claims but, at the same time, she feared that this attitude could cause a recurrence of the anorexia.

Underneath these reasons, one could read her real request: she wanted to understand what had caused the mess of the preceding years, what she had done wrong, for what reason her daughter was so obstinately reproaching her. She had intense feelings of guilt about this matter. The problem of her daughter's illness in the past as well as Julia's present difficulties were presented by her in linear, causal terms, and limited to the mother–daughter dyad.

The danger of a linear punctuation is that it can easily become fossilized; it can also very readily be read in reverse, in this case from "I, your mother, have made mistakes with you, my daughter" (or "I'm the guilty one and you are the victim") to "you, daugher, tyrannize me and are in the wrong" (or "you are the guilty one and I am the victim"). It appears that, as long as the problem is seen from a linear point of view, it is impossible to get out of this oscillation between "I am the cause" and "you are the cause." However, in this case, we were not trying to find out who was the guilty party. How should one do so in a story in which all of the characters appear to be victims and losers?

At this point the goal of therapy was to look for possible alternative readings of events, which Julia could make use of in order to construct new, more functional premises.

An unforeseen event, which reminded Julia of old family games, made it possible to start this restructuring process. Julia was invited to return to the job she had left the year before at the explicit request of her husband, when Deborah had become symptomatic.

Therapist: How do you intend to organize things to go back to work?

Julia: Well, I imagine that I'll have a rather heavy load, because I'll have to cook the noonday meal in the morning before leaving for work, and I'll have to do the various household chores when I get home in the evening. But I'm not very worried. After all, I'm not the only woman in the world who has an outside job!

Therapist: How do you think that your husband and your daughter will manage without you?

Julia: It won't be a problem for my husband. All he needs is to find lunch ready, because right afterwards he's busy giving private lessons. As to my daughter . . . I don't know . . . she's unpredictable. . . .

Therapist: What worries you about your daughter?

Julia: It's that I don't know how she'll react to my absence. Since she left the hospital, she has been spending practically all of her time with me. I can't do anything without her tagging along. Before doing anything, she always asks my advice or else she has me accompany her. The truth is that my daughter is crucifying me! For example, when she's going to change her clothes, or telephone a friend, or go out to buy bread, she won't do it without first asking me what I think she ought to do. . . . But then, she doesn't accept any answer I give her. When she heard about my job, she became even more nervous. . . . I have the feeling that she doesn't really accept the situation and that she'll upset everything. This time I can't simply throw up the job after 2 months like before. If I do, well I can just kiss this job good-bye forever!

Therapist: Are you afraid that the same thing that happened last year will happen again?

Julia: No, not exactly, because I don't think that Deborah will become anorexic again. But if she decides that I shouldn't go to work, then she'll really kick up a fuss!

Therapist: Do you think that you can't manage to resist the pressure that your daughter might put on you?

Julia: This time I'm really determined. But I am rather anxious about it—that I can't deny.

Therapist: What do you think that your husband thinks about this problem?

Julia: We've spoken about it, and he assured me that he'd help, because he knows that I really care about this job.

Therapist: Do you think that your husband is going to be able to manage this situation by himself—I mean, if your daughter really decides to retaliate?

Julia: Well, I hope so . . . because, after all, he understands that she has some unbearable ways of acting, that she treats us like puppets. . . . (Her voice breaks.) We're not dealing with an illness anymore. She simply enjoys ruling over us with an iron rod. It's as if she were doing this on purpose to see me suffer. I've told you: I feel like she's nailing me to the cross! (Julia begins to cry.)

Therapist: It appears as if you think that your daughter has a specific plan. Is that what you think?

Julia: Yes, something like that . . . I don't know, it's difficult to explain. . . .

Therapist: Tell me what you feel, what you sense.

Julia: I feel that I'm a target. It's as if she were doing everything possible to wear me down, otherwise it doesn't make sense. (Her voice becomes more agitated.) She's a tyrant. She leaves me no freedom of movement. Wherever I am, she's always there. It's as if she didn't want me to be by myself. . . . If only I knew why she behaves this way with me, what it is that she wants to punish me for—because she's not like this with her father, even though lately she has been a bit arrogant with him. . . .

Therapist: So, it seems to you that it's as if Deborah were acting a part in a play in which the main characters are a mother and her daughter, right?

Julia (smiling): Yes.

Therapist: And does the father have a role in this play?

Julia: I don't think so. . . . I'm her only target.

Therapist: But why do you think Deborah has to do this? Have you any ideas?

Julia: I don't know. . . . I think that she can't stand me, that she wants to punish me for something . . . but I don't know what I've done that's so terrible!

Therapist: So, do you think that she does it because she's being nasty?

Julia: No, but I think she's being obstinate, very obstinate.

Therapist: Have you ever thought that Deborah might be going through all this effort on behalf of somebody?

Julia (after a long silence): What do you mean? How? One of us?

Therapist: No. I'm just making hypotheses. What I mean is that usually when people are stubborn or obstinate, they have good reasons for it. But, on the other hand, you don't think that Deborah is acting like this because she's nasty by nature, nor because you, Julia, have made some unpardonable mistake. You've spoken to me of the stubbornness, hardness, and persistence of your daughter's behavior. All of this makes me think of a fight, but one fights that stubbornly for something or somebody very important, to defend an ideal or a loved one or one's own dignity. Don't you think that it's possible that your daughter is sacrificing her relationship with you for somebody or something, for some sort of just cause?

Julia (hesitantly): I don't know . . . I'd never thought of that . . . I need time for reflection.

Therapist: I can see that. We could continue to discuss this next time, if you'd like.

The therapist's introduction of an alternative hypothesis began to crack Julia's explanatory hypotheses, in particular, the causal connection that she had made between her being bad and the behavior of her daughter. The patient was thus able to consider a larger range of possible meanings of events in which she had been and was still the main person involved, and thus arrived at the point of revising and reconstructing her particular system of beliefs.

At the following session, Julia told the therapist that she had had a long talk with her husband, with whom she had discussed the previous session. She had been bewildered by the hypothesis that the therapist had formulated. For days she thought of little else. If Deborah is fighting a battle, if she is giving it her all (the therapist had actually said "sacrificing"), then her husband had to be informed, and the two parents should discuss this together.

Julia: I wanted to know what my husband thought of it—the hypothesis was suggestive, but it was still just an idea. Well, do you know what he said? He said that maybe Deborah was doing all of this for him, because maybe she had understood that he had some problems with regard to my work. He confessed that last year, when he had asked me to stop work because he couldn't manage Deborah alone at home, maybe he, without being completely aware of it at the time, was actually completely blocking me from going to work at all. He told me that he was jealous that I had found a job and that I was enthusiastic about it, so satisfied, while he can't stand the work he's doing. And now, even though he's happy for me, he's suffering. Maybe Deborah understood all of this. . . .

Therapist: It's quite possible that Deborah sensed that it was better for her father if you, Julia, did not begin to go to work again. Maybe she thought that as long as there was somebody to guide and care for him, then that person was useful and important, but if she "loses" her mother, then what's to be done?

The restructuring of Julia's premises had a reverberating effect on the structural system of her family, and ended up cracking and dismantling the myth. A radical recalibration of family relationships, roles, and areas of responsibility of each member ensued. Julia, although unsure and anxious, began her job. Not long after this talk between husband and wife, Julia's husband decided to seek psychotherapy to resolve his personal problems, which had been, up to that point, covered up by the family myth. Almost miraculously, Deborah stopped concentrating her energies on controlling her mother, and established with Julia a correct relationship of adolescent child (which she was) to mother. Julia's therapy lasted for a year and a half.

STRIVING FOR PERSONAL IDENTITY

A case that we found particularly interesting is that of a 27-year-old man who came to our Center because his mother, worried about Michael's repeated threats of suicide, had requested family therapy.

Michael had twice before attempted individual therapy. However, he had stopped both times after two or three sessions. After carefully evaluating the material regarding Michael's life history and his interpersonal relations which came to light during the two consultation sessions, the therapists tended toward a diagnosis of a borderline personality disorder. Michael clearly showed at least seven of the eight characteristics listed for that disorder in *DSM-III*: impulsiveness, intense and unstable interpersonal relations, emotional instability, difficulty in tolerating being alone, self-damaging behavior, and chronic feelings of emptiness and boredom.

Michael had abandoned his high school studies at the age of 16. Technically, he worked in his father's firm, but he did not actually hold any definite position: he simply "helped" his father. In fact, he was often not there, going in only every now and then, without any particular commitment. He spent the rest of the time sleeping, seeing girlfriends (however, his romantic attachments were always very unstable), and, off and on, rebuilding vintage cars. He often overindulged in alcohol and spent large sums of money (which his father lavished on him without the knowledge of his mother) on foolish purchases. Michael had frequent explosions of anger, accompanied by fits of crying and angry assertions that his parents did not understand him. His parents seemed to be in perpetual disagreement over how they should act with their son. His mother appeared to be rigid and intolerant. Michael's father seemed too tolerant and yielding, while, at the same time, he complained of his son's lack of commitment. He had established an exclusive relationship with his son, taking full responsiblity for his upbringing. He blocked every move his wife made toward participation. As a consequence, Michael's mother found it easy to attach to him all of the responsibility for their failure to raise their son properly.

During the two consultation sessions, the patient appeared to be ambivalent toward his father's omissions. On the one hand, he expressed intolerance of his father's control over him, but on the other, Michael seemed to be very much attached to him and defended his father every time it seemed to him that his father was being attacked. Toward his mother, he seemed unresponsive and emotionally detached.

The therapy session extract presented below will give the reader an idea of the extent to which Michael's father interfered in his son's life as well as of the son's lack of independence.

Therapist: What particular functions do you perform at work?

Michael: I don't have a specific job. I stay with my father. We go together to see clients. I stay in the car and wait for him.

Therapist: Do you have any decision-making power in the firm?

Michael: My father is a nondelegator, and he doesn't leave anything to anybody else. However, I have my own ideas and I would like to put them into action.

Therapist: Have you ever thought of changing jobs and leaving your father's firm?

Michael: I wouldn't be able to get another job. I don't know how to do anything else. . . . Well, maybe I could be a street sweeper or a garbageman.

Therapist: How do you think you father would react if you were to leave the firm?

Michael: It would be the end for him. He can't be without me. He would be lost . . . he wouldn't be able to work by himself.

Therapist: But you just said that you don't have any particular job and that you have no particular specialty. How would things change for your father?

Michael: That's not the point. He always asks my opinion even if he ends up doing whatever he has in mind.

Therapist: Your opinion about what?

Michael: About clients, for example. He asks for my impressions of people.

Therapist: And does he take them into account?

Michael (unsure): Well, to some extent . . . and then, he always wants to talk about work with me. When I come back home at night, even if it's two in the morning, he insists on telling me what happened at work during the day—things that we've done together—I get angry about this and act nastily towards him.

Therapist: Does your father stay up waiting for you?

Michael: No, but sometimes he wakes up during the night. If he sees the light on in my room, he comes in.

Therapist: What does he do? Knock and ask if he can come in?

Michael: No, he just enters—my door is open. (anticipating the therapist's question): No, it doesn't bother me. It's not a problem. I leave it open.

Therapist: Michael, don't you have any area that is yours alone? I don't mean that it has to be a physical space—I mean something that you have all to yourself, that you don't share with anybody.

Michael (hesitantly): My work tools—at least I try to keep them to myself, but they always take them away and then I have to look all over the place at work to find them. Then, there's also my hobby of cars. I take them apart and reconstruct them by myself. I spend a lot of time at it. (becoming more animated) The other day I had an argument with my father because we're reconstructing an off-the-road vehicle, and he's determined to be the expert. On this subject, he's not better than me . . . but he always wants to teach me things, even about cars.

Therapist: How is it that you're doing this together? Does your father have the same hobby?

Michael (a bit ill at ease): Recently, he proposed that we buy this off-the-road vehicle and work on it together to fix it up.

Therapist: Why did your father come up with this idea?

Michael: Well, he wants to share something with me that's not just work—he wants to share everything with me.

Therapist: How do you feel about this?

Michael (ill at ease): Well, I guess I understand him—I'm very attached to him—but sometimes I feel he's stifling me.

Therapist: What did you think of this proposal of working on the car together?

Michael (a bit irritated): Well, I too like to do things with him. I respect him very much. But it bothers me that he insists that he's the expert, because I know more about cars than he does.

Therapist: What does your mother think about this shared activity?

Michael: I don't know. I have no idea. I never talk with my mother.

Therapist: If you tried, couldn't you imagine what she'd think?

Michael: I guess that she'd probably disapprove.

The problem of his parents' disagreement over him was a huge burden for Michael—he felt responsible for their constant squabbles. He expressed concern particularly for his father, because lately the tense situation at home had been adversely affecting the latter's physical health. During the consultation sessions, Michael's father had repeatedly stated that Michael had always divided the couple. It seemed clear that the son was being exploited by his parents within their relationship as a couple. In order to free Michael from his feelings of guilt, it was necessary to demolish his linear cause-and-effect association between his parents' marriage problems and himself. This operation was carried out via the use of a very strong therapeutic tool that systemic therapists have at their disposal: reframing.

Michael: I've always been the main subject of my parents' arguments, or, rather, maybe the only one. I can't remember them ever arguing about anything else, even when I was a child. My mother has always reproached my father for being too softhearted with me; she always says that he is too protective of me.

Therapist: What do you think of this idea of your mother's?

Michael: I don't know. Lately, I've been quite miserable. I don't have any motivation for doing anything else. My mother would like me to have a proper job—she wants me not to ask my father for money—but I can't keep my spending within the limits of my salary. I never make it to the end of the month. My father's allowed me to use his credit cards, but that really got my mother mad when she found out about it.

Therapist: How did your mother find out about it?

Michael: My father told her. He always says, "Don't tell your mother—she'll get mad," and then he goes and tells her.

Therapist: Why do you think he tells her if he knows that she disapproves?

Michael (embarrassed): I don't know.

Therapist: And if I were to ask your mother, what do you think she'd say?

Michael: I haven't the slightest idea.

Therapist: What else do your parents talk about, other than you?

Michael: Nothing, I imagine.

Therapist: Do you think it's possible that your mother and father don't have anything to say to each other?

Michael (in a somewhat irritated tone of voice): I don't know . . . it's none of my business.

Therapist: It seems to me that this subject makes you uncomfortable. How come?

Michael: I don't like speaking about their business. Their affairs have nothing to do with me.

Therapist: But your parents talk about your business, they argue about you.

Michael: Yes, but I don't like to talk about them.

Therapist: Maybe you don't want to talk about their strained relations. You said before that your parents have always discussed matters concerning you and very often these discussions became fights. You've said, time and time again, and in the previous sessions as well, that you've always been their favorite topic of both conversation and argument—perhaps the only topic. You've also expressed various times the idea that you're the cause of your parents' disharmony, that you've pulled them apart. . . .

Michael (in a weak voice): Yes.

Therapist: Haven't you ever thought that maybe instead of having divided them, you've contributed to keeping them together?

Michael listens in silence.

Therapist: Maybe, if you hadn't been around to be talked about, maybe your parents would really have had nothing to say to each other. You have made them talk. You have kept their relationship alive. You've worked hard at this. You've been really good at it. Do you think that it's possible that when you were still a child you became aware that your parents didn't have the ideal marriage—the kind all children have in mind for their parents—and that this made you very unhappy? It might have been that you therefore have sacrificed yourself for all of these years by sticking yourself there in the middle, not to keep them apart but rather to keep them together.

Michael begins to cry quietly.

Therapist: Maybe your parents can only stay together on the condition that you give them a valid reason to continue to fight with each other. . . .

Michael (after a long pause): I never thought about that. . . . Do you mean that I kept them occupied for all these years?

Therapist: Yes. I mean that if it hadn't been for you, maybe your parents wouldn't have known what to say to each other for quite some time—and you picked up on this. Children are often like very sensitive thermometers which can detect a cooling off in their parents' relationship.

Michael: I've often wondered how come they ever got married to each other. . . . My mother always talks about her moral principles, so I think she'd never consider a separation from my father. Sometimes he allows her to yell at him as if he were a child, but when it has to do with me, he knows how to impose his will. Maybe I'm useful to him. (Michael becomes more animated.) Maybe you're right . . . I never thought of that.

Therapist: How do you think that you could get out of this situation?

Michael: I haven't the slightest idea.

Therapist: You've been paying an awfully high price with this sacrifice of yours. You've given up your aspirations (which certainly you had and still have), your independence, your right to decide what to do with your life. . . .

Michael begins to cry again.

Therapist: Maybe it's time for you to drop that role. It's time that your parents look squarely at their marriage relationship without your mediation and begin to communicate about other things, if this is possible. You have to take care of yourself and begin to make your own life. . . .

Michael (in a small voice): I wouldn't know where to begin. . . .

Therapist: We can begin to think about it together.

Starting from this reframing, a 2-year course of therapy (which had its ups and downs) was begun. At the conclusion of therapy, Michael had made considerable progress. He had changed jobs and was running a branch of an automobile accessories firm together with a friend of his. At home he had carved out a niche for himself. At that time he was considering the possibility of living on his own, even though he was still struggling with economic problems since he still had trouble keeping his spending for nonessentials within his means. Michael's interpersonal relationships were still not stable, and therefore he had not formed any significant relationships. Michael had neither threatened suicide again nor engaged in any more self-destructive behavior.

An interesting note: About a year after Michael started individual therapy, his parents returned to our Center to request couples therapy. Michael made especially noticeable progress in therapy when his parents began couples therapy.

AN UNACCEPTABLE EMOTION

Eighteen-year-old Alice, an only child, came to individual therapy after the conclusion of family therapy, which had been initiated due to her being ill with anorexia nervosa. The recommendation for individual therapy had been made by the family therapy team in the final session of family therapy.

The eating disorder showed a distinct improvement as therapy progressed. By the time family therapy was concluded, Alice had regained her health, at least physically. She had gained a substantial amount of weight and had reestablished appropriate eating habits. Her menstrual cycle had resumed, after an interruption of several months.

Nonetheless, Alice still had a number of problems, which had been brought to light by family therapy. However, because of the way family therapy is set up, these crucial points had not been confronted and resolved.

When Alice came to family therapy, she complained of a pervasive sense of dissatisfaction. She felt depressed and discontent with the life that she led. She had very few friends because she refused all invitations and any contact with her classmates, although, in spite of her refusals, her company was continually sought. It appeared that her studies were her only remaining interest. However, in contrast to the past, she found it very difficult to maintain the same standard of perfection that had characterized her brilliant scholastic career up until this time. She was even considering going to work after getting her high-school diploma rather than going on with her studies. However, these were simply aspects of more complex problems, which had roots in her family history.

When Alice was in elementary school, she was cared for after school by her maternal aunt, since her mother had a full-time job. Gradually, a very close bond was created between the two families. As they had many interests in common, they organized trips on the weekends and always spent their vacations together.

Alice would spend the balance of the day after school at her aunt's house. She would do her homework and then play with her two cousins until her parents came to pick her up in the evening. She got along very well with her two cousins, a boy her age and a girl just slightly younger. The two families came to call them the "three siblings," recalling a familiar children's song with those same words. Alice's aunt was always considered Alice's second mother rather than a relative to whom the temporary care of Alice had been entrusted. She had been given carte blanche, and this contributed to her gradually beginning to make decisions about her niece on her own. Alice's parents had never appeared to object to the way things were going, or, at any rate, they never openly declared their opinions about the situation.

Actually, during the course of family therapy, Alice's mother spoke about how it had irritated her that her sister had taken her place so thoroughly. Nonetheless, she and her husband had decided to remain silent about this, because they were afraid of offending her and because, after all, she was of great help in minding their daughter.

The family of her aunt and uncle remained very important in Alice's mind even after she had grown up enough to take care of herself and no longer spent her afternoons with them. When Alice became ill with anorexia, it was the aunt who advised Alice's parents which specialists to contact and how they should deal with the dire situation of a hunger strike whose meaning nobody was able to fathom. It was at this time that Alice's mother, who had been openly accused by her sister of maternal incompetence and irresponsibility, opportunely broke off relations with her sister and her brother-in-law. Nonetheless, Alice's father continued to visit his in-laws, in part because he did not fully agree with the position that his wife took, and in part because he was particularly fond of his nephew.

From childhood on, Alice had had to deal with four parents: two mothers who were engaged in a silent battle for the place of honor in Alice's heart, and two fathers who were merely present in the background of the battlefield.

With regard to her parents, her feelings were ever-changing. She looked upon them with tender affection, justifying the weakness that had kept them from opposing the overbearing intrusion of her aunt into their lives. But, at the same time, she also felt deeply hurt, and she could not manage to pardon them for having allowed this to happen, for having delegated to other persons, albeit relatives, the job of bringing her up.

There was this same sort of alternation with regard to Alice's alliances with her parents. At intervals, she felt solidly behind her mother against her father. Her father had abandoned both of them, preferring Alice's aunt and cousins. On the other hand, the fact remained that even Alice's mother had abandoned her when she was a child, letting the aunt assume the role of mother.

Family therapy had redefined the limits of Alice's family, had given back to the parents their roles and powers, and had finally removed the confusion about the significant persons in Alice's life. Nonetheless, the deep feelings that had been called up because of this confusion had yet to be confronted. Although the just-concluded family therapy had brought to light the family games of which Alice had been the unwitting central character, Alice was still not completely able to recognize and tolerate the emotions she had felt in those situations.

In this individual therapy, the restructuring of the patient's premises or system of beliefs did not play a central role the way it usually does in our model. This task had already been accomplished in family therapy. This therapy was for dealing with emotions. These emotions were hidden and unexpressed, denied but nonetheless felt, and for this reason they were a source of suffering. We have chosen this case to demonstrate how, even within a model which is inclined toward the analysis of relationships and of behaviors, there is still room for working on emotions and feelings. We hope that, notwithstanding the sterility of written extracts, the reader will nevertheless be able to sense the intensity of the emotions that were addressed, explored, and discussed in the therapy room.

Alice: This week nothing in particular happened except that one evening there was a violent argument between my mother and my father. At the end of it, my mother left the house and didn't return for a good 2 hours.

Therapist: Is this the first time that your mother has ever done anything like that?

Alice: Yes. She'd never done that before, and all pandemonium broke loose!

Therapist: You seem very impressed by this. How come?

Alice: Well, it wasn't very pleasant. We were all scared. My father looked for her everywhere. He telephoned everywhere, too. But he couldn't find her anywhere. I was awfully frightened. I couldn't imagine where she had gone, and besides it was nighttime, too. . . .

Therapist: You were very frightened. And your father, how do you think he took it?

Alice: He was more angry than frightened, especially because he had to go out and look for her, and he didn't even find her. So we remained home waiting for her. Every now and then my father would sputter. I felt just awful—I felt guilty about my mother—I didn't know what to do. . . .

Therapist: If your mother left after a fight with your father, why did *you* feel guilty about your mother?

Alice: Because my parents were arguing about me. My father had come home and found my mother and me in the sulks, because we had had one of our usual quarrels. So he started saying that he could not stand seeing us always on edge, that this wasn't what life should be like, that he worked all day and didn't like coming home to such a stifling atmosphere—well, things like this. So they began to fight and they kept at it for quite some time, even though I asked them to stop—but when my father flies off the handle, it's difficult to get him to stop. . . . (Alice's voice cracks.) And then . . . then my mother left, saying that she was leaving . . . that she was fed up with everything and everybody and that she was leaving for good. . . . Well, that's how it was.

Therapist: A lot of people say things like that when they are angry or when they fight.

Alice: I know. My mother must have said that a thousand times before, but she had never before actually left the house. I knew that she would return. She's not the kind of person who just picks up and leaves her family, but I still felt miserable. . . . (Alice begins to cry.)

Therapist: What happened after that?

Alice: Nothing. (a long pause) Things settled down, just like that—by themselves, without our talking about them, at least between my mother and me. (Alice continues crying.)

Therapist: What is it that makes you feel so miserable?

Alice: I don't know. I just can't deal with these scenes at home any more! I'm miserable for days about it. But, in the end, I feel bad to see my mother suffer on my account!

Therapist: Do you mean the episode that you've been talking about? Was that an occasion on which your mother suffered on account of you?

Alice: Yes, but that's also true in general. When my mother came home, my father forced her to go to my room and talk with me, but she didn't want to . . . but then he convinced her . . . and she said to me, "What do I have to do to make you understand that I love you?" (Alice begins to sob.)

Therapist: How come it was so important for your father that you and your mother talk?

Alice: Because he can't stand seeing long faces at home. He wants us to resolve issues, without there being any aftermath. . . .

Therapist: What do you think your mother thought of the fact that your father forced her—to use your words—to go to your room to talk with you?

Alice: Well, I guess that she would have thought that my father, as usual, prefers for things to calm down right away. But she—I think that she did it simply to avoid further problems—but she certainly wasn't convinced—she wouldn't have come to speak with me of her own free will, and she could have spared herself this. . . .

Therapist: Would you have appreciated that more?

Alice (remains silent for a moment, then answers in a small voice): Yes, I think so.

Therapist: A few moments ago, you said that you feel that you're the cause of what happened at your house the other night. Who else, do you think, thinks the same thing?

Alice: Everybody—my father, my mother. They always tell me, "From the time that you became ill, we don't get along any more."

Therapist: And how do you answer that?

Alice: I don't say anything. Sometimes it makes me angry, but at other times I think that it's true.

Therapist: The other night you thought that it really was true—that it was your fault that your father and mother had argued, and that your mother went off and left. I don't understand why, even now, you prefer to think that between your mother and your father there was never any problem, apart from your anorexia.

Alice (in an annoyed tone of voice): My father and mother never argued—at least not like this!

Therapist: What do you think your mother was thinking when she went to your room and said those words of love?

Alice: Maybe she was thinking that she makes a great effort to meet me halfway, while I do a lot less. . . . She thinks that I'm not aware of that, but I know that she does everything that she can to get along with me.

Therapist: And how did you answer her?

Alice: I didn't say anything. I was sitting at my desk, reading a book, and I didn't even lift up my head, because I didn't know what to say. . . .

Therapist: But, how come your mother wants to know whether or not her own daughter understands that she is loved?

Alice (crying): I don't know. It's something that I just can't understand. . . .

Therapist: To me it seems that more than anything, this question makes you suffer.

Alice: Yes . . . but it's always the same story . . . I have to make declarations of love to everybody, otherwise . . . they're not content. I have to be happier, to enjoy myself. I have to make an effort to go out, to have more friends . . . to try to be more approachable. . . . Well, I'm supposed to do all these things. . . .

Therapist: Let's go back to love. It seems to me that this is a problem between you and your mother. Were there any other times when your mother has asked questions similar to this?

Alice: Yes, when I was little, when they would bring me to my aunt's house every now and then she would say something like that. . . . But I never took much notice—I didn't spend much time with my mother, because she worked. I would stay at my aunt's, and after school I would play with my cousins, but when my mother arrived to pick me up, my mood would change. . . .

Therapist: Do you remember how that happened?

Alice: Well, I'm not so sure . . . but I remember that my aunt would tell me that—but maybe I noticed it, too.

Therapist: But didn't you ever wonder why your aunt would call to your attention that your mood would change when your mother arrived?

Alice: No, I never thought about it—but it really annoyed me when my aunt would say that in front of my cousins, so I would pretend not to have heard her. The fact is that I didn't have much fun with my mother. It isn't that she was a dictator, but she was always on edge and she used to yell at me because I always made a big mess. . . .

Therapist: And so you preferred to stay at your aunt's. . . .

Alice (a bit perplexed): Maybe.

Therapist: Do you find it so strange that a child of 7 or 8 years old would enjoy playing with her cousins more than being taken to task for being messy? But probably this is not the main reason that you perhaps preferred staying at your aunt's house. . . .

Alice (half talking to herself): I don't know what to say. . . .

Therapist: Does it bother you to talk about this?

Alice: No, but we're talking about things that happened such a long time ago . . . that I don't know if . . . I don't remember very much. . . .

Therapist: That's OK. We're simply making suppositions. It's not so important to reconstruct the facts—I'm merely interested in what you think about it. What do you think that a child of that age thinks about a mother who works all day long and has her daughter go to her aunt's house after school?

Alice: Maybe that her mother could stay at home instead of going to work. . . .

Therapist: Do you think that that's what you thought when you were a child? That you would have wanted your mother to stay at home with you?

Alice: I would see my aunt who prepared snacks for us and took us to the park, and I would wonder why Mom didn't also do that? What had I done to her? I couldn't figure out why she couldn't give up her work and stay at home like other mothers.

Therapist: Were you angry with your mother?

Alice: What are you talking about! I was a little kid, and I couldn't understand that she had to work and that it was important for a woman to have her own interests.

Therapist: Now you are thinking like an 18-year-old, but we are talking about a little girl! What does a child of 8 feel?

Alice: I don't know . . . I don't remember. . . .

Therapist: All right. I've known children who were in the same situation. Let me tell you how they felt. They told me that they felt let down, abandoned, in a vacuum without hope of getting out. And all of them—yes, all of them—felt resentful toward their mothers. I think that you, too, felt that way. Isn't that so?

Alice (crying): But that isn't very nice! It wasn't her fault!

Therapist: Of course not! But how could you have known that? You simply felt that your mother had decided not to stay with you. The reasons for the things that adults do don't interest children! I would be very surprised if you had felt anything else, seeing that your aunt stayed at home with her children, while your mother did not. You said before that you didn't remember well, but I think that you know very well what you felt about your mother deep in your heart, because it is a feeling that has been with you for a long time, that every now and then comes to the surface and peeks out, even though you wish that it wouldn't happen. (A long silence follows.) I realize that this is very painful for you—it must be a terrible thing for you. You think that it is reprehensible for a little child to feel angry with her parents. Well, let me tell you that anger is one of the first emotions that children feel. Anything and everything that doesn't satisfy their needs sparks off anger, especially in situations in which they can't understand why Dad or Mom isn't there with them. And it is certainly the case when the people who take care of the child do not transmit to the child the secure feeling that the situation is only temporary, that Mom is going to come back and everything will be the same, and that nothing has changed.

Alice: I remember that sometimes, when I would make Mom angry, she would say, "So, it's true that you love your aunt more than you love me!" Then I would feel bad, because it wasn't true . . . but I really felt guilty.

Therapist: Was it sort of like being found out? Is that what you mean?

Alice: Yes, precisely . . . it was terrible for me. Now I know that it wasn't easy even for my mother—there were all of those problems with my aunt—but I didn't know that, and it bothered me that she would always scold me . . . because for me it was she who didn't love me and not the contrary!

Therapist: All of this still makes you feel miserable, right?

Alice: Yes, that's right.

Therapist: Maybe that's the reason why you are so inclined to take the blame for your parents' squabbles and feel such distress when your mother says those things—is that so?

Alice: I think maybe it's like feeling unmasked twice.

Therapist: I think that you should not let your mother say such things and also that you should not allow your parents to say that they fight only because of you. All three of you know that this is not so!

In the next few sessions Alice began to speak about her feelings. She spoke about episodes during the time she was anorexic that she felt were examples of her continual search for confirmation of her mother's love. When she considered this clearly, she felt that these attempts to test her mother's love for her arose from the feeling of anger that she had constantly felt while she was growing up. She described her aim as in essence saying to her mother, "Now let's see if you're with me this time, or if you still don't love me."

Finally, the moment came when Alice began to experience the effect of recognizable and accepted emotions, which could be either negative or positive, when she recognized the fact that feelings are not unchangeable things that necessarily jeopardize relationships and freeze them in an immutable pattern.

It was the beginning of a period of emotional growth for the patient. She was finally able to free herself and the important persons in her life from feelings of blame. When Alice finished therapy at the age of 20, she was no longer isolating herself from social contacts as she had in the past. Her relationship with her parents (in particular, with her mother) appeared to be well balanced and no longer contaminated by factors of past history.

A MANIPULATED RELATIONSHIP

Twenty-three-year-old Miranda was the only child of a late-middle-aged couple. Her father was wholly dedicated to his work and spent very little time at home, while her mother, a homemaker, was almost completely in symbiosis with Miranda. Miranda had left school after finishing junior high and had never held a job. She spent all of her time at home and had no significant social relationships outside of the family. She went out only with her mother, and she also went on vacation with her mother alone. Miranda's father spent his vacation at home on the pretext of having work to do. Miranda could hardly think of any examples of the three of them spending time together. On the rare occasions when her parents went out together, Miranda stayed at home alone.

For a couple of years, this young woman had had various episodes of bulimia, followed by self-induced vomiting. However, already since puberty, Miranda had had body-image problems. She considered herself to be ugly and fat, even though she was quite pretty and was barely a few pounds over her ideal weight. She had had cosmetic surgery a number of times, with the complicity of her mother, but without her father's knowing anything about it.

Accompanied by her mother, Miranda came to our Center to ask for individual therapy, saying that she wished to lose weight before going to the seaside for vacation. She said that she had a closetful of new clothes that she had never worn because of her weight, and that she had finally decided that she was going to wear them. Naturally, neither Miranda nor her mother had told her father about applying for therapy. However, Miranda said that she was sure that her father would neither have approved of this initiative nor have ever agreed to take part in family therapy.

During the course of the first session, Miranda brought up an idea she had been toying with recently: she was considering enrolling in a vocational school for office workers, a project that she said caused her mother much anxiety. Miranda's mother insisted that her daughter "recover" before taking on any type of scholastic or work commitment. Lately, there had been a number of discussions about this subject. Miranda's father had been excluded from these, or, in Miranda's opinion, he had avoided being involved in them. Miranda always read her father's behavior in terms of a lack of interest or a voluntary exclusion from anything that concerned her.

From the very first session, it was clear that it was necessary to repunctuate the various situations with alternative proposals for reading them. One of the reasons for this was that it was evident that Miranda's mother actively excluded her husband from involvement in their daughter's life, which she herself had literally cornered. The therapist was particularly struck by the fact that Miranda had never directly heard for herself her father's opinions on anything that concerned her—they were always related to her by her mother, who acted as a go-between for communications between father and daughter.

Thus, the therapist began to suspect that Miranda's mother had always impeded the establishment of any relationship between father and daughter. Of course, no systemic therapist can avoid imagining that in this the mother had the complicity of the father, through some sort of tacit agreement that would have regulated the couple's relationship pattern.

The mother's maneuvers with regard to this emerged from Miranda's reports of various family situations.

Miranda: During the week, I eat with just my mother for company. She doesn't bother me very much. Even if I eat only sweets, she doesn't say anything. Sometimes it is she who buys them for me when she goes food shopping.

Therapist: Doesn't your father ever eat with you?

Miranda: No. He doesn't come home from work at midday and he returns home very late in the evening. So, there's only Sunday. . . .

Therapist: So, on Sunday, you all eat together!

Miranda: Well, no. I don't eat with them. It bothers me if he watches me when I eat because he always has something to say. For him whatever I eat isn't proper.

Therapist: So, you don't eat with your parents on Sunday, right?

Miranda: No, I don't. I take what I want to eat before they sit down at the table, and I bring my plate down to my grandmother's place. She lives on the floor below us. However, she's not there when I go there, because she goes to my aunt's house to eat.

Therapist: How did you think up this idea?

Miranda (speaking in a somewhat uncertain voice): Actually, it was my mother's idea. She knows that certain things that my father says bother me. She understands me. She's not like my father! When she said that I could go down to my grandmother's house to eat without being disturbed, it seemed like a good idea to me.

Therapist: How did this decision go over with your father?

Miranda: I don't know. I imagine it went over OK—the less I'm around him, the better it is. My mother says that I make him nervous.

Therapist: You've never spoken directly about this with your father?

Miranda: Would you believe it! I don't speak with my father. My mother would have explained it to him.

Therapist: Didn't you ask your mother how your father reacted?

Miranda: No. Anyway, I already know what he's like.

Therapist: Well, then, how do you think he reacted?

Miranda: No reaction. I told you. At least he eats in peace.

Therapist: How do you think that your mother communicated to your father your decision to go down to eat at your grandmother's? What reason would she have given for your decision?

Miranda: I don't know . . . she'd have told him some story or other . . . she might have said that it was the doctor who suggested it . . . to get me to eat.

Therapist: Have there been other times when your mother told stories to your father about you?

Miranda (heatedly): Of course! He doesn't believe that I have an ailment. He says that I'm simply undisciplined and acting up, and that it's my mother's fault because she's always looking after me—but the doctor knows that I suffer from bulimia.

Therapist: How do you know that this is what your father thinks if you don't speak to each other?

Miranda: My mother tells me! Sometimes he really dishes it out to her, and then she lets off steam with me.

Therapist: Does she ever vent her anger on your father?

Miranda: No. He's got a bad temper. My mother always says that it if weren't for me . . .

Therapist: If it weren't for you, what?

Miranda: No . . . well . . . she just talks like that when she's angry—but usually she and my father get along OK.

Therapist: Miranda, do you think your father thinks along the same lines as you do about your relationship with him? I mean, if I were to ask him to speak to me about you, what would he say?

Miranda (after a rather long pause): I don't know . . . he wouldn't know what to tell you . . . he'd tell you that we never speak with each other, we just barely say "hello" and "good-bye."

Therapist: Mmm, Miranda, do you think that for your father things are fine that way or that he's unhappy that the situation is like this?

Miranda: No. For him it's fine like this. I don't appeal to him, nor does he appeal to me.

Therapist: And does your mother like the situation being this way?

Miranda (hesitantly): Well, no, I think she doesn't like it. She tries to remedy the situation by being both mother and father to me, because it's as if he didn't exist.

Therapist: Don't you think it might just be the opposite way around? That your father is unhappy about the situation and that it's just fine with your mother?

Miranda (puzzled): What do you mean?

Therapist: What I mean is, how can you be so sure that your father wouldn't like to have a different kind of relationship with you?

Miranda: Well, he wouldn't act the way he does . . . he'd behave differently.

Therapist (beginning to reframe): Maybe he simply can't act in any other way. Maybe he thinks that it would make your mother unhappy if he did. . . .

Miranda (her face lighting up with sudden comprehension): Why would it make her unhappy?

Therapist: I don't know, . . . I'm hypothesizing. Do you have any ideas?

Miranda is silent for a long time.

Therapist: Maybe he thinks that if your mother didn't act as the go-between for you both she would feel left out, that she would suffer. . . .

Miranda (hesitantly): It might be that she's jealous about me. . . . In fact, she is a bit possessive. . . . She's always only occupied herself with me. . . .

(Miranda then launched on a long digression about her childhood, using this maneuver to change the subject from the dangerous field that the therapist had entered on. The therapist, judging it premature to insist upon this subject, decided to put off a full-fledged reframing intervention until Miranda was ready for it.)

Work was immediately begun on the indirect communication between father and daughter. Miranda tended to describe this as absence of communication. It was obvious that the patient equated communication with verbal interchanges, which, in fact, were almost nonexistent between the two of them. Therefore, the therapist decided to prompt Miranda to think about things her father did that involved both of them as well as interpersonal situations in which both of them were involved, encouraging her to see them as meaningful. After a rather difficult beginning, it was possible to determine material upon which to work to point Miranda in that direction. One seemingly banal episode that Miranda related attracted the attention of the therapist because it clearly revealed Miranda's mother's position. In discussing this episode with Miranda, the therapist took the opportunity to introduce a reframing punctuation, which was amply worked on afterwards.

Miranda: I like animals very much—all of them, even pigeons. My mother says that pigeons are dangerous, because they carry disease. A good many pigeons come to our terrace and they dirty it up, so my mother chases them away (giggles) and I, instead, try to feed them. Usually she pretends not to notice, but the other day she really blew her top!

Therapist: How come?

Miranda: The other day—it was Sunday—while my mother cleared the table, I gathered up the crumbs and went out on the terrace to give them to the pigeons. In fact, maybe I did go overboard—it really was full of pigeons—also because my father noticed and went to get more bread. After a while, my mother came out and saw all those pigeons—what a disaster! She started to yell—I said I'd clean up after them—I'd never seen her so mad about pigeons ever before! She even began to yell at my father.

Therapist: So, what did your father do?

Miranda: Nothing, he went off to the coffee bar.

Therapist: What did your father say while the two of you were feeding the pigeons? What did you talk about?

Miranda: Nothing. We didn't talk.

Therapist: Were there other times when you and your father would feed the pigeons together?

Miranda: Yes, when I was a child—my father liked animals, too. When I was a teenager—probably I was about 13—he bought me a dog. I had it for just a short time, then I had to give it away because we lived in an apartment. My mother always yelled because the dog dirtied up the place, and she also said that I had to study and I wasted too much time with the dog. I remember that I was really sad and cried a lot when we gave it away. . . .

Therapist: Was your father also sad about giving away the dog?

Miranda: I think so. He, too, liked the dog. He used to play with the dog and we would give the dog a bath. . . .

Therapist: Miranda, the other day, when your father saw you feeding the pigeons and he went to join you, do you think that maybe he wanted to communicate something to you? I mean, even if he hadn't spoken, maybe he wanted to have some sort of contact with you again like, for example, when you were a child and the two of you had in common your love of animals. Don't you think that it is possible to communicate without using words?

Miranda (with a tone of uncertainty): Well, I guess so. . . .

Therapist: Try to think of other situations in which your father might have been trying to be together with you, to have some sort of communication with you.

Miranda (after a rather long period of silence): That's difficult. . . . Perhaps when we used to play with the dog, but that was a long time ago. . . .

Therapist: Of course, The dog was probably a vehicle of communication for the two of you.

Miranda: Yes. But then we gave it away, and afterwards we didn't do anything together any more.

Therapist: You said that your mother didn't like the dog, that you gave it away for that reason.

Miranda: Yes. My mother doesn't like animals.

Therapist: Do you think that it was only for that reason? Or because something else may have bothered her?

Miranda (hesitantly): Well, maybe the fact that I was together with my father. . . . Do you think that it might also have been this?

Therapist: What do you think?

Miranda: Well, my mother was always a bit jealous about me . . . but I never thought she was about sharing me with my father. . . . However, she really would get mad when we spent a lot of time with the dog.

Therapist: Maybe she felt a bit left out of the things that you had in common with your father, like, for instance, your interest in the dog. Maybe she felt that the two of you being together was sort of dangerous for her. Maybe your mother had concentrated all of her time and energy on you and feared she might lose you. Maybe your father understood this, and to avoid hurting her, backed away. However, that wouldn't mean that your father wouldn't like to have something in common with you, or that he didn't care about you. . . .

Miranda (beginning to cry silently): I'd always thought that my mother was unhappy when she saw how my father acted toward me . . . and now . . . maybe it was she who kept us apart!

Therapist: Probably she did this unintentionally, unconsciously, but the effect would still have been the same. Your mother's not to blame. Sometimes, when a person devotes all of her time and energy to another person, and all of her hopes and aspirations are connected with this one particular person, it can happen that, unconsciously, she might tend to encroach on all areas, to intrude in the affairs and relationships of this person, to monopolize him or her. . . .

Miranda: Yes, I guess it was like that. She's always given all her time to me. If I weren't there, what would she do? My father at least has his work—he can manage without me—but maybe he, too, would like to have me. . . .

Therapist: I think that you really ought to consider this possibility seriously.

The therapist's rereading of the situation prompted the patient to consider the behavior of her parents and the roles they played in her life from another point of view. This rereading was intended to orient Miranda toward revaluing the image of her father while not destroying the image she had of her mother. This permitted her to accept as positive sentiments even the distortions of the love of her mother.

Miranda's therapy was concluded after 20 months. At that time, Miranda was attending the second year of a vocational night school. Miranda had also already for some time been working as a clerk in a stationery shop. Her relationship with her mother had become somewhat strained while Miranda was in therapy because the young woman had almost immediately begun to demand that her mother recognize her autonomy. At the beginning, the therapist's support was indispensable, but gradually Miranda became capable of bearing by herself the burden of the conflictual relationship with her mother. Miranda's relationship with her father gradually improved considerably as Miranda continued to make efforts to understand his timid communicative indications or at least to interpret her father's behavior as attempts at communication with her.

With regard to her bulimia, Miranda learned to eat in a more or less correct and regular manner. The symptom showed up only occasionally, at times of unusual stress, and then only in an attenuated manner, for example, she would eat a whole box of cookies or a box of chocolates at one time, but she limited herself to that.

AN UNFINISHED THERAPY

The last case that we will present is that of 21-year-old Gerald, an only child, who was a second-year law student. At the time of his entering therapy, he had been suffering for about a year from attacks of panic and anxiety crises, which made class attendance difficult for him and greatly limited his social life.

Gerald contacted us through his mother, a physiotherapist. However, he followed up by telephoning us to ask for an appointment.

His father, an accountant in a bank, was not informed of the request for therapy, since Gerald believed that his father preferred to ignore his son's symptoms, even though he was aware of them. Father and son never discussed the symptoms together. According to Gerald, his father avoided this anxiety-producing problem because it worried him to such an extent.

For 4 months, Gerald had been working in a sports equipment store. He spoke about this occupation in a rather immodest manner, almost as if this occupation were a profession of great prestige. Gerald's parents had not given their approval to their son's decision to go to work. However, they were not opposed to it, although they felt that this might limit the amount of time Gerald could devote to his studies (causing him to take more time to complete the work for his degree). Gerald had been a brilliant student in junior high school, but his performance in high school and at the university had fallen off considerably.

Gerald described his relationship with both of his parents in positive terms, specifying, however, the differences. His mother was described as being the more active parent where decision making was concerned, whereas his father was more marginal in that respect, although he still played a part in his son's life. From Gerald's description, the situation did not seem to present great problems. However, he seemed to be very uncomfortable when it came to talking about his life and, particularly, speaking about his parents. When the therapist pointed this out to him, Gerald rationalized his reticence by saying that he tended to be reserved by nature and that he did not particularly enjoy speaking about his life.

Another subject about which Gerald was particularly reticent was his love affair with a girl of whom his parents did not approve (because her family belonged to a lower socioeconomic class than their family). This relationship had lasted for 2 years before having been broken off by Gerald about a year previous to the beginning of therapy. Gerald had felt that this relationship was an important one, and he expressed bitterness about breaking up. However, he rationalized this too, saying that he had made this decision because he realized that his parents were right, that Elena simply was not the girl for him.

Gerald was very worried about his symptoms and the practical implications of them for the various areas of his life. He constantly wanted to be reassured by his therapist that he was "normal." The only area in which the patient seemed to be free of problems was that of his work.

In the first session, a fact came out that provided a starting point for an investigation of Gerald's parents' expectations of him and of their sacrifices for him. Although Gerald's family belonged to the middle class, his parents' aspirations were clearly higher. They wanted the best of everything for their son: a university degree, a prestigious profession, a higher standard of living. Gerald said that he was in agreement with his parents' attitudes about his future. However, his tone of voice, his choice of words, his lack of emotional involvement, and a rather resigned attitude gave the therapist the feeling that Gerald merely agreed passively to his parents' preestablished plan for him. It appeared that Gerald was simply repeating, without any enthusiasm, a lesson he had obediently learned. The first few therapy sessions were utilized for verifying the therapist's hypothesis of the patient's covert disagreement with his parents' ideas and for stimulating him to recognize this disagreement and state it openly.

Gerald: Some days I just don't have enough willpower to stick with my books. I don't feel like simply studying and doing nothing else. I'm scared that I won't succeed in completing the work for my degree. . . .

Therapist: You've said that several times before. How come you're afraid that you won't manage to get your degree?

Gerald: Because I know myself. I'm weak-willed.

Therapist: Would you feel very sorry if you didn't finish your studies?

Gerald: Well, it's not so much that. It's that I would disappoint my parents.

Therapist: Do you think that they also have doubts about your determination? Do they also think that you won't succeed?

Gerald: No, I don't think so. They've never said so. They're convinced that I'll get my degree.

Therapist: How come you chose to go to college?

Gerald: Well, I, too, understand that a college degree is an important thing, that it will help me find a good job when I graduate.

Therapist: This seems like a very good reason, very sensible. But are you sure that this decision, that you've made with your mind, is in agreement with your own inclinations, your own wishes, deep down in your heart? I remember that when you were speaking about your choice of major you said that you were not particularly interested in law, but rather that you had simply agreed with your parents that this field opened up interesting possibilities of employment. If you had been able to choose whatever you wanted to do without having had to make a rational choice, what would you have done?

Gerald: I don't know. I never thought about it. I knew that I was going to go to college.

Therapist: Try to think about it now. If you could choose on the basis of your innermost desires, what would you do?

Gerald (hesitatingly): Nothing special. I like the work that I am doing now. I get to be with people, I feel comfortable doing it, and I could make a career of it. I think I would quit college. . . .

Therapist: So, if it depended only on you, you would quit school?

Gerald (in a low voice): Yes.

Therapist: But you don't do that because of your parents. . . .

Gerald: Right.

Therapist: If you decided to do this, what would they do?

Gerald: Nothing, but they would be very displeased—they've made many sacrifices for me. And besides, they're right. It is clearly better for me to continue with my studies.

Therapist: You also told me that they were right in their judgment of your girlfriend. . . .

Gerald: Little by little, I came to understand that she wasn't right for me, that we were too different in various ways. . . .

Therapist: Give me an example.

Gerald: Well, she had no ambition . . . and there were also too many differences in the way we were brought up. . . .

Therapist: And what did the two of you have in common? If you saw each other for 2 years, you must have had something in common.

Gerald (becoming more animated): We both enjoyed the things that we did together, like going to the movies and skiing. We had the same free-time interests, but our ways of thinking were a bit different.

Therapist: You said that your parents didn't like this girl very much. . . .

Gerald: Although later they had almost come to accept her. . . . It was I who made the decision to break up with her!

Therapist: What type of girl do you think *would* please your parents? What qualifications would she have to have?

Gerald: I couldn't say . . . nothing in particular. . . .

Therapist (deciding to give her reading of the situation): Gerald, when you speak, I get the impression that, instead of speaking about yourself, you are speaking about another person, about a stranger. You have the detached air of somebody who is speaking of things that have nothing to do with him.

Gerald is perplexed and remains silent.

Therapist: We are talking about your life! About your hopes, about your plans for the future, about your current experiences—all of this in extremely rational terms. What about your feelings? (a rather long pause) You speak to me unemotionally about decisions regarding you, you make a great effort to convince me that you're not angry with your parents, that you agree with their ideas, that you feel understood, but you don't convince me. I see that you are trying to adapt to an image of yourself that isn't really you, in order to conform to the ideal model of a son, which, however you could never recognize as truly being you, because you are a different person! Maybe you are afraid of the thought of finding out that you are not that person, but, on the other hand, while you make a great effort to adapt yourself to that model, you feel inadequate, you feel that you still don't please your parents. Besides, this effort is exacting a high price: it makes you anxious, it makes you suffer. Maybe you ought to begin to realize this, to begin to think about it. I leave that as an assignment to you for the next session.

This extract is a good example of an active intervention on the part of a therapist. The therapist's map is proposed to the patient by communicating perceptions, impressions, suppositions. This strategy has the potential for putting into motion a drastic reframing of the situation, although there is a certain risk of induction. Therefore, it is necessary that the therapist have great breadth of experience and feel certain that he/she is able to trust his/her intuition. Obviously, it is necessary to have gathered a sufficient amount of data during the course of observation to back up one's intuitions. Below is an extract from the next session. It shows the orienting and restructuring effect of the therapist's intervention.

Gerald: All week long I've been thinking about what you said to me last time, and many memories have come back to me—things that I hadn't thought about for quite some time. . . .

Therapist: For example?

Gerald: Well, for example, when I was a school child, my mother would always tell me that I was not to disappoint my father. I did well in junior high school, but then in high school, mainly the first year, I got a few failing grades. I remember that my father did not punish me, or even yell at me, but he would repeat time and time again that I should be grateful for the fact that I had the good fortune to be able to go to school and that I must not waste this opportunity, otherwise I would be making my parents very sad. He would always say the same thing—I think I would have preferred to have been punished or yelled at, and have the matter closed. And whenever I would get good marks, they'd say that I had simply done my duty. . . . Thinking it over again, I remember having always felt this heavy burden, the responsibility of having to succeed at any cost. It was simply expected that I would be able to manage to do well—it was my obligation to make them happy. I simply could not be a mediocre student. But, in fact, I was mediocre, and sometimes I was ashamed because I didn't put forth much effort and I knew very well that my parents attached great importance to this matter . . . and the same thing is happening now with my university examinations—they expect me to pass all the examinations with good marks.

Therapist: Do you feel that your parents don't approve of you, that they don't accept you?

Gerald: On the whole, yes, I'd say that. I think that they would like a different kind of son, especially my father.

Therapist: Different in what way?

Gerald: Mmm . . . maybe more ambitious, more committed to his studies. I remember that when I finished junior high school, I wanted to go to a technical high school and study electrotechnics with a schoolmate of mine, who was also a close friend, but my parents didn't allow me to do that. I said that I wanted to be an electrician when I grew up, but they said that this work was not suitable for me. They said that I had the opportunity to study and to have aspirations of a better occupation. Thinking it over again, I believe that they were terribly disappointed with me at that time, when I said that I wanted to become an electrician. If I had said that I wanted to become an engineer . . .

Therapist: And the job at which you work now? You told me that your parents weren't terribly happy with the fact that you are working.

Gerald: They certainly aren't happy about it. They say that I am wasting time that I need for my studies. But I have the impression that it's not only that—maybe what they don't like is the fact that I am working as a sales clerk.

Therapist: Have they ever told you that?

Gerald: No. They never speak frankly, but I know that they are not pleased with what I do. (a long pause) It was also that way with Elena . . . maybe I was wrong to break up with her. . . .

Therapist: What do you mean by "it was also that way"?

Gerald: I mean that I felt that it was not only Elena herself that my parents didn't like but also her family—her father was a truck driver. Once my mother asked me, "What is it that you see in her?" You are right, I've always tried to adapt myself to their wishes, while sacrificing my own, and to be as they wanted me to be, but I haven't succeeded. . . .

Thus, Gerald began to look at the situation from a different viewpoint, recognizing his own personal aspirations and starting to take responsibility for his own life. He is beginning to insist that his parents recognize his needs as legitimate, even if they are in opposition with their expectations; and he is also starting to resist their attempts to manipulate him.

Therapy is still going on, but is probably close to being terminated. After 10 months of treatment, the symptoms are very much reduced, although not completely eliminated. Gerald's social life has changed for the better. He has begun to go out again with his friends, although he doesn't feel completely at ease yet. Gerald has begun seriously to consider the possibility of giving up his studies and devoting his time completely to his job, which he still finds very satisfying.

REFERENCES

Agazzi, E. (1978). *I Sistemi Tra Scienza Filosofia*. Torino, Italy: Societă Editrice Italiana.

Andolfi, M. (1979). *Family Therapy: An Interactional Approach*. New York: Plenum.

Ashby, W. R. (1956). *An Introduction to Cybernetics*. London: Chapman & Hall.

_____ (1964). The set theory of mechanism and homeostasis. *General Systems* 9:92–120.

Atlan, H. (1979). *Entre la Cristal et la Fumée*. Paris: Editions du Seuil.

Bateson, G. (1972). *Steps to an Ecology of Mind*. New York: Ballantine.

_____ (1979). *Mind and Nature: A Necessary Unity*. New York: Dutton.

Bennun, I. (1986). Evaluating family therapy: a comparison of the Milan and problem solving approach. *Journal of Family Therapy* 8:80–93.

Berger , P. L., and Luckmann, T. (1966). *The Social Construction of Reality*. Garden City, NY: Doubleday.

Bertalanffy, L. von (1967). *Robots, Men, and Minds*. New York: Braziller.

_____ (1969). *General System Theory*. New York: Braziller.

_____ (1971). *Il Sistema Uomo*. Milan: Isedi.

Bocchi, G., and Ceruti, M., eds. (1985). *La Sfida della complessità*. Milan: Feltrinelli.

Boscolo, L., Cecchin, G., Hoffman, L., and Penn, P. (1987). *Milan Systemic Therapy*. New York: Harper & Row.

Buckley, W., ed. (1967). *Sociology and Modern Systems Theory*. Englewood Cliffs, NJ: Prentice Hall.

———— (1968). *Modern Systems Research for the Behavioural Scientist*. Chicago: Aldine.

Burbatti, G., and Formenti, L. (1988). *The Milan Approach to Family Therapy*. Northvale, NJ: Jason Aronson.

Caillè, P. (1987). Le modele systemique des relations humaines ou l'hypothese de l'autonomie creative. *Terapie Familiale* 8:19–30.

Cecchin, G. (1987a). Hypothesizing, circularity and neutrality revisited: an invitation to curiosity. *Family Process* 26:405–413.

———— (1987b). La famille peut-elle être considerée comme un systeme autopoietique. *Terapie Familiale* 8:99–106.

Ceruti, M. (1986). *Il Vincolo e la Possibilitá*. Milan: Feltrinelli.

Cronen, V. E., and Pearce, W. B. (1985). Toward an explanation of how the Milan method works: an invitation to systemic epistemology and the evolution of family systems. In *Applications of Systemic Family Therapy: The Milan Approach*, ed. D. Campell and R. Prater, pp. 102–153. London: Grune & Stratton.

Delattre, P. (1984). *Teoria dei sistemi ed Epistemologia*. Torino, Italy: Einaudi.

Dell, P. (1982). Beyond homeostasis: toward a concept of coherence. *Family Process* 21:21–41.

Denton, W. (1990). A family systems analysis of DSM-III-R. *Journal of Marital and Family Therapy* 16:113–125.

Elkaim, M. (1981). Non equilibrium, change and chance in family therapy. *Journal of Marital and Family Therapy* 7:291–297.

Ferreira, A. (1963). Family myth and homeostasis. *Archives of General Psychiatry* 9:457–463.

Foerster, H. von (1962). *Principles of Self Organisation*. New York: Pergamon.

———— (1981). *Observing Systems*. Seaside, CA: Intersystems.

Gibney, P. (1990). Is there a place for psychiatric diagnosis in family therapy? *Australian and New Zealand Journal of Family Therapy* 11:229–234.

Gollan, J. (1988). On second order family therapy. *Family Process* 27:51–65.

Gray, W., Duhl, F. J., and Rizzo, N. D., eds. (1969). *General Systems Theory and Psychiatry*. Boston: Little, Brown.

Haire, M., ed. (1959). *Modern Organisation Theory*. New York: Wiley.

Haken, W. (1985). L'approccio della sinergetica al problema dei distemi complessi. In *La Sfida della Complessità*, ed. G. Bocchi and M. Ceruti, pp. 194–207. Milan: Feltrinelli.

Haley, J. (1963). *Strategies of Psychotherapy*. New York: Grune & Stratton.

———— (1971). *Changing Families: A Family Therapy Reader*. New York: Grune & Stratton.

Haley, J., and Hoffman, L. (1968). *Techniques of Family Therapy*. New York: Basic Books.

Hall, A. D., and Fagen, R. E. (1956). Definition of system. *General Systems* 1:18.

Harari, E. (1990). Diagnosis and family therapy: "traditional" psychiatry and the concepts of disease and diagnosis. *Australian and New Zealand Journal of Family Therapy* 11:160–165.

Harré, R., and Secord, P. F. (1972). *The Explanation of Social Behaviour*. Oxford, England: Basil Blackwell.

Hoffman L. (1971). Deviation-amplifying processes in natural groups. In *Changing Families: A Family Therapy Reader*. New York: Grune & Stratton.

———— (1981). *Foundations of Family Therapy*. New York: Basic Books.

Jackson, D. D. (1957). The question of family homeostasis. *The Psychiatric Quarterly Supplement* 31:79–90.

———— (1965a). Family rules: marital quid pro quo. *Archives of General Psychiatry* 12:589–594.

———— (1965b). The study of the family *Family Process* 4:1–20.

Jackson, D. D., and Weakland, J. H. (1961). On theory, technique and results. *Psychiatry* 24(suppl.):30–45.

Keeney, B. P. (1979). Ecosystemic epistemology: an alternative paradigm for diagnosis. *Family Process* 18:117–129.

———— (1982). What is an epistemology of family therapy? *Family Process* 21:153–168.

Keeney, B. P., and Ross, J. M. (1985). *Mind in Therapy: Constructing Systemic Family Therapies*. New York: Basic Books.

Laszlo, E. (1973). *Introduction to System Philosophy*. New York: Harper Torchbooks.

Livet, P. (1983). *La fascination de l'auto-organisation*. In *L'auto-organisation: de la Phisique au Politique*, ed. P. Dumouchel and G. P. Dupuy, pp. 50–63. Paris: Seuil.

Loriedo, C., Angiolari, C., and De Francisci, A. (1989). La terapia individuale sistemica. *Terapia Familiare* 31:13–25.

Lovaas, O. I. (1987). Behavioural treatment and normal educational and intellectual functioning in young autistic children. *Journal of Consulting and Clinical Psychology* 55:3–9.

MacKinnon, L. (1983). Contrasting strategic and Milan therapies. *Family Process* 22:425–438.

Maruyama, M. (1968). The second cybernetics: deviation-amplifying mutual causal processes. In *Modern Systems Research for the Beha-*

vioural Scientist, ed. W. Buckley, pp. 304–313. Chicago: Aldine.

Maturana, H. (1980). Man and society. In *Autopoiesis, Communication and Society*, ed. F. Benseler, P. Heijl, and W. H. Köck, pp. 11–30. Frankfurt, Germany: Verlag.

———— (1988). Biology of language: the epistemology of reality. In *Psychology and Biology of Language and Thought*, ed. G. A. Miller, and E. Lenneberg, pp. 27–63. New York: Academic.

Maturana, H., and Varela, F. (1980). *Autopoiesis and Cognition: The Realisation of the Living*. Dordrecht, Holland: Reidel.

———— (1985). *The Tree of Knowledge*. Boston: New Science Library.

McCulloch, W. (1965). *Embodiments of the Mind*. Cambridge, MA: M.I.T. Press.

McKinnon, L. K., and James, K. (1987). The Milan systemic approach: Theory and practice. *Australian and New Zealand Journal of Family Therapy* 8:89–98.

McLeod, W. R. (1988). Epistemology and constructivism: some implications for therapy. *Australian and New Zealand Journal of Family Therapy* 9:9–16.

Mead, G. H. (1934). *Mind, Self, and Society*. Chicago: University of Chicago Press.

Miller, J. G. (1965a). Living systems: basic concepts. *Behavioral Sciences* 10:193–237.

———— (1965b). Living systems: structure and process. *Behavioral Sciences* 10:337–379.

———— (1965c). Living systems: cross-level hypotheses. *Behavioral Sciences* 10:380–411.

———— (1978). *La Teoria Generale Dei Sistemi Viventi*. Milan: Angeli.

Morin, E. (1973). *Teorie Dell'evento*. Milan: Bompiani.

———— (1977). *La Methode. Vol. I: La Nature de la Nature*. Paris: Editions du Seuil.

———— (1980). *La Methode. Vol. II: La Vie de la Vie*. Paris: Editions du Seuil.

———— (1986). *La Methode. Vol. III: La Connaissance de la Connaisance*. Paris: Editions du Seuil.

Neumann, J. von, and Morgenstern, O. (1947). *Theory of Games and Economic Behaviour*. Princeton, NJ: Princeton University Press.

———— (1958). Computer and the brain. Yale University Hepsa Helly Silliman Memorial lectures. New Haven: Unpublished.

Pagels, H. R. (1982). *The Cosmic Code*. New York: Simon & Schuster.

Penn, P. (1982). Circular questioning. *Family Process* 21:267–280.

Prekop, J. (1984). Elforgsrate det therapie durch festhalten. *Kinderartz* 9:1170.

Prigogine, I. (1980). *From Being to Becoming*. San Francisco: Freeman.

Prigogine, I., and Stengers, I (1979). *La Nouvelle Alliance: Metamorphose de la Science.* Paris: Gallimard.

Rodgers, R. (1977). The family life cycle concept: past, present and future. In *Family Life Cycle in European Society,* ed. J. Cousenier, pp. 80–105. Paris: Mouton.

Ruesch, J., and Bateson, G. (1951). *Communication: The Social Matrix of Psychiatry.* New York: W. W. Norton.

Russell, G. F. M., Szmukler, G. I., Dare, C., and Eisler, I. (1987). An evaluation of family therapy in anorexia nervosa and bulimia nervosa. *Archives of General Psychiatry* 44:1047–1056.

Selvini Palazzoli, M. (1980). Why a long interval between sessions? In *Dimensions of Family Therapy,* ed. M. Andolfi and I. Zwerling, pp. 161–169. New York: Guilford.

———— (1985). *Cronaca Di Una Ricerca.* Rome: La Nuova Italia Scientifica.

———— (1986). Towards a general model of psychotic family games. *Journal of Marital and Family Therapy* 12:339–349.

Selvini Palazzoli, M., Boscolo, L., Cecchin, G., and Prata, G. (1977a). Family rituals: a powerful tool in family therapy. *Family Process* 16:445–453.

———— (1977b). La prima seduta di una terapia familiare sistemica. *Terapia Familiare* 2:5–13.

———— (1978). *Paradox and Counterparadox.* New York: Jason Aronson.

———— (1980a). Hypothesizing, circularity, neutrality. *Family Process* 19:3–12.

———— (1980b). The problem of the referring person. *Journal of Marital and Family Therapy* 6:3–9.

———— (1983). *Behind the Scenes of the Organization.* New York: Pantheon.

Selvini Palazzoli, M., Cirillo, S., Selvini M., and Sorrentino, A. M. (1989a). *Family Games.* New York: W. W. Norton.

———— (1989b). L'individuo nel gioco. Parte seconda: strategie terapeutiche e progresso della conoscenza. *Terapie Familiare* 31:65–72.

Selvini Palazzoli, M., and Prata, G. (1981). Insidie della terapia familiare. *Terapia Familiare* 10:7–17.

Selvini Palazzoli, M., and Selvini, M. (1991). Team consultation: an indispensable tool for the progress of knowledge. Ways of fostering and promoting its creative potential. *Journal of Family Therapy* 13:51–63.

Sluzky, C. E. (1986). A minimal map of cybernetics. *Networker,* May–June 1985, p. 26.

Sluzky, C. E., and Beavin, J. (1965). *Symmetry and Complementarity:*

The Interactional View. New York: W. W. Norton.

Sluzky, C. E., Beavin, J., Tarnopolski, A., and Vernon, E. (1967). *Transactional Disqualifications: The Interactional View.* New York: W. W. Norton.

Sluzky, C. E., and Ramson, D. C. (1976). *Double Bind: The Foundation of the Communicational Approach to the Family.* New York: Grune & Stratton.

Speer, D. C. (1970). Family systems: morphostasis and morphogenesis, or is homeostasis enough? *Family Process* 9:259–278.

Stengers, I. (1983). A propos de l'epistemologie cibernetique. *Cahiers Critiques de Therapie Familiale et de Pratiques de Reseaux,* 7:93–102.

Taylor, F. W. (1947). *Principles of Scientific Management.* New York: Harter Bros.

Toner, B. B., Garfinkel, B. E., and Garner, D. M. (1986). Long-term follow-up of anorexia nervosa. *Psychosomatic Medicine* 48:520–529.

Varela, F. (1979). *Principles of Biological Autonomy.* New York: Elsevier.

_____ (1983). L'auto-organization: de l'apparence au mechanisme. In *L'auto-organisation de la Phisique au Politique,* ed. P. Dumouchel and G. P. Dupuy, pp. 147–175. Paris: Seuil.

_____ (1984). Living ways of sense making. In *Disorder and Order,* ed. P. Livingstone. Stanford, CA: ANMA.

_____ (1989). Reflections on the circulation of concepts between a biology of cognition and systemic family therapy. *Family Process* 28:15–26.

Watzlawick, P., Beavin, J. H., and Jackson D. D. (1967). *Pragmatics of Human Communication.* New York: Norton.

Watzlawick, P., and Weakland, J. H., eds. (1977). *The Interactional View.* New York: W. W. Norton.

Watzlawick, P., Weakland, J. H., and Fisch, R. (1974). *Change: Principles of Problem Formation and Problem Resolution.* New York: W. W. Norton.

Whitaker, C. (1989). *Midnight Musings of a Family Therapist.* New York: W. W. Norton.

Whitaker, C., and Napier, A. Y. (1981). *Il Crogliolo Della Famiglia.* Rome: Astrolabio.

Whitehead, A. N., and Russell, B. (1910–1913). *Principia Matematica.* Cambridge, England: Cambridge University Press.

Wiener, N. (1965). *Cybernetics, or Control and Communication in the Animal and the Machine.* Cambridge, MA: M.I.T. Press.

Zappella, M. (1987). *I Bambini Autistici, L'Holding e la Famiglia.* Rome: La Nuova Italia Scientifica.

INDEX

About the Authors

Guido Burbatti, M.D., Ph.D., is Director of the Center for the Study of Family Therapy Niguarda-Ca' Granda Hospital, director of the Family Therapy Postgraduate School of the Gregory Bateson Center, and Director of the "Olison Project": Advanced Technologies in Psychotherapy and the Socio-medical Field, at the Gregory Bateson Institute, all in Milan, Italy.

Ivana Castoldi holds a degree in physics from the Università degli Studi of Milan, and a degree in psychology from the Università degli Studi of Padua. She also holds a master's degree in family therapy from the Postgraduate School of the Gregory Bateson Center in Milan, Italy, where she is currently a professor.

Lucia Maggi holds a degree in psychology from the Università degli Studi of Padua and a master's degree in family therapy from the Postgraduate School of the Gregory Bateson Center in Milan, where she is currently a professor.